D1097064

Fort Ross
The Ship in The Shadow

Roger McAfee

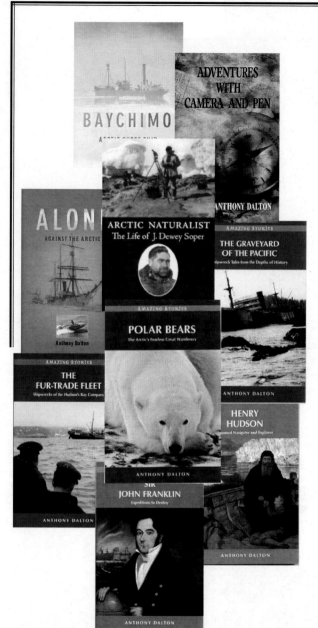

FORT ROSS, The Ship in the Shadows, is a welcome addition to the library of Canada's Arctic nautical history. The author tells the ship's story factually; without flowery embellishments. M.V. *Fort Ross* was a working ship in the Hudson's Bay Company's extensive fleet. Her domain was the Arctic, arguably the most difficult waters in which to navigate. *Fort Ross* acquitted herself well season after season in the ice, but there are gaps in her record and author Roger McAfee has done his best to explore those missing months. In an addendum, he argues that the ship could have been the first to navigate the North-West Passage and he does so convincingly. He also reminds us of the importance of protecting Canada's Arctic sovereignty and puts forward strong warnings for all Canadians – from private citizens to the powers in Ottawa – to be aware the importance of our territorial rights.

Anthony Dalton, author of seven non-fiction books on the Arctic.

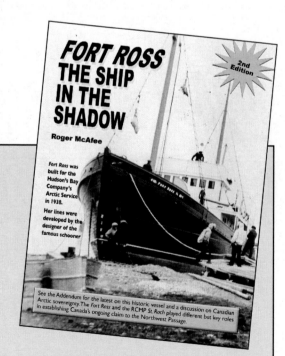

Fort Ross was built for the Hudson's Bay Company's Arctic Service in 1938. Her lines were developed by the designer of the famous schooner

See the Addendum for the latest on this historic vessel and a discussion on Canadian Arctic sovereignty. The *Fort Ross* and the RCMP *St. Roch* played different but key roles in establishing Canada's ongoing claim to the Northwest Passage.

SECOND EDITION

ISBN 0-9686853-8-2
Vancouver, B.C., April 2002, June 2016

Cover photo courtesy of Hudson's Bay Archives.
Production: Pacific Marine Publishing.
Printed in Canada on recycled paper

Table of Contents

Foreword

The Arctic is a region that is seen as harsh, unyielding, and, as Stan Rogers sang in "Northwest Passage," a land both wild and savage. It is far more complex, and the environmental conditions are but one aspect of a place that has featured powerfully in human history for millennia.

The story and culture of the Inuit are the longest lasting aspect of humanity's time in the Arctic. Another is the saga of the quest for a northwest passage, a centuries long quest that for many scholars ends in 1903-1905 when Roald Amundsen and his crew became the first Europeans to sail across the top of the world in the tiny wooden-hulled Gjoa.

As Canadians know, the passage was then not only part of Canada, but it was not empty. In addition to the Inuit, there were others who lived up there – Mounties, missionaries, Hudson's Bay Company factors, traders – and a variety of ships ranging from whalers and trading ships. No one had tried to go all the way through. That had been the enterprise of governments and explorers, at times ending tragically. For those making a living or doing their job, working the waters of the passage, in and around local communities was their reality of navigating the fabled Northwest Passage.

The next celebrated navigation came because men were sent north to work, not to explore or establish a new achievement in the annals of human endeavor. The voyage of RCMP St. Roch of 1940-1942 and 1944 are celebrated, but for me, it is the work that St. Roch performed under the command of Henry Larsen and his crew from 1929 to 1948 that stands out. That service to the people of the north and to Canada is often overshadowed by the ever-present fascinating with "the passage."

Also there, and often ignored, were the hard working vessels and crews of the Hudson's Bay Company. Some, like Nascopie, are better

Across the Top of the World is a tale of the quest for the fabled Northwest Passage that lured bold adventurers to the icy Arctic. They risked and sometimes lost their lives in search of a sea route across the top of the world, connecting Europe with Asia and its riches.

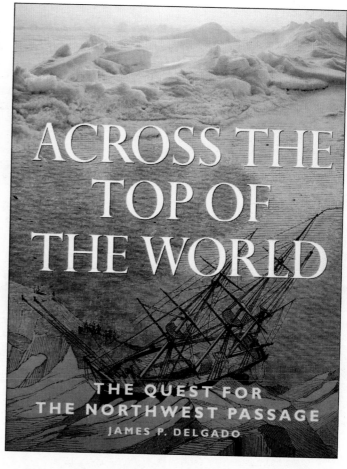

known than others. Others, like Fort Ross, are less known. Roger McAfee has set out to rectify that with this account of that ship and its time in the Arctic. McAfee brings the history of that vessel to life and adds to the knowledge of the Arctic and the Northwest Passage during the time the vessel operated in Canada's north.

While I don't agree with McAfee's conclusion about how the vessel got from the west coast to the east coast in 1941, his argument is sure to lead to more discussion and research into the vessels operating in the Arctic during the 1930s and 1940s. This is an area that has long needed more said about it. It to me is far more the essential aspect of Arctic maritime endeavor than better known and failed expeditions at the cost of ships and lives. That being said, those epics of ambition, travail and sacrifice also resonate, but they should not dominate the discussion. I believe that this book offers more and provokes more research

and discussion. For me, ultimately, it is not the story of who made it through the passage, it is the ongoing saga of human endeavour in the north, as well as at sea, and in exploring this, at its regular, dare we say mundane, we get at what history truly is. It is the story of people existing and persisting, day to day, often in extraordinary circumstances that they take as just another day on the job.

–*James P. Delgado, PhD*

Fort Ross
The Ship in The Shadow
About the Author

The author is a former journalist, lawyer and strategist who has been involved in boating for more than seven decades. As with many families in Northern Ontario and Northwestern Quebec, Roger's introduction to boating started when he leaned to fish with his dad.

As he grew up his Scout troop built a number of wooden rowboats, with the help of various Scouting fathers. As outboard motors grew more powerful waterskiing and boat racing were added to the watersports. For Roger SCUBA diving was also added to the list and he ultimately became a certified SCUBA instructor.

In 1959 he left the East and headed for Vancouver where he attended the University of British Columbia. Despite his best efforts and involvement in driving rally cars, flying, the student newspaper, student politics and SCUBA diving he graduated with a couple of university degrees and practiced law for a couple of decades. He also spent a lot of time boating.

While messing around with boats he modified a small outboard fishing boat which he used as a plug to make half a dozen small high speed cathedral hull fishing boats for family and friends. He then developed one of the first outboard brackets on the West Coast that allowed him to mount his 150 HP outboard two feet behind the boat and four inches higher than the traditionally mounted motor well set up. This resulted in a 20 percent speed increase at wide open throttle or a 24 percent reduction in fuel consumption at cruise.

He and a group of friends bought a 62 foot ex-RAF crash boat they used as a dive boat and as a safety boat for the UBC engineers' entry in the formerly world famous, now defunct, Nanaimo to Vancouver Bathtub Race. That boat was equipped with a propane stove and the group wanted to use a diesel stove but the vessel construction did not allow traditional diesel smoke stack to exit through the overhead. Roger developed a smoke extractor that allowed the stove pipe to exhaust out through the hull of the vessel immediately beside the stove.

The crash boat was sold and the group acquired a 65 foot steel hulled power boat. The rebuilding of that boat led to Roger's first marine related book – The Steel Hull – a book on steel hull repair and maintenance.

Many years ago, in 1969 to be exact, Roger, along with another group of friends, brought a boat, owned by a Vancouver marina and charter boat operator, from Canada's east coast, through Panama back to Vancouver. The vessel poked around the Caribbean where the diving was great and the beer and wine inexpensive As bottle of Johnny Walker Black could, in those days, be had out of bond for $1.41 a bottle and Mumm Extra Dry Champagne cost $3.00 a bottle!

When Roger and his friends took that trip on the Fort Ross they knew only that the vessel had been a Hudson's Bay Company ship In fact there were brass letter embedded in the helm wheel that read "HB Co. 1939." However no one on the trip realized, at that time they were on an historic vessel. This book is about the Fort Ross and that trip.

Roger has continued his involvement in the marine field as a free lance writer. He has also been a member of the Board of Directors of Boating Writers International and has been, a number of times, a member of the Innovation Awards judging panel a both IBEX and the Miami International Boat Show.

He is the chair of the judging panel for the Pacific Yachting Best In Show Awards, given out annually at the time of the Vancouver International Boat Show. He is also the referee on the Pacific Yachting Pacific Challenge. That event is a timed challenge to power boats to circumnavigate Vancouver Island with only the fuel they have on board when they leave the start/finish line in Victoria.

Vancouver, B.C. March 2016

Fort Ross *launching 1938. Photo: Hudson's Bay Archives, Provincial Archives of Manitoba.*

The Ship in The Shadow

Introduction

to the 2016 edition

In 1969, I and a group of young divers, both men and women, were scheduled to spend a couple of weeks diving in the unbelievably pristine waters of Barkley Sound, on the west coast of British Columbia's Vancouver Island.

Barkley Sound was, at that time, the "dream dive" for experienced temperate water divers from all over the world. Rollers from the open Pacific Ocean crashed along the coast keeping the waters stirred up and creating ideal conditions for fish and shell fish.

It was about January and we had been planning the trip aboard a vessel then called *Thomas Crosby IV*, a former United Church mission boat being operated as a charter vessel by Bob Blackmore, a marina operator in Vancouver. We had, for a number of years, been chartering the vessel for diving in the Strait of Georgia, the body of water between the B.C. mainland and Vancouver Island.

One day my phone rang and Bob called to advise he was in the process of buying another boat and that it looked like the Barkley Sound trip was off:
"However," he said, "if I get the other boat, how would you guys like to help me bring it to Vancouver?"

To say I was disappointed was an understatement. However, Bob had been incredibly good to our group. We were the only group he allowed to charter his boat for diving.

"I'm sure we would be happy to help," I said, trying to hide my disappointment "Where is the new boat located?" I expected it to be somewhere on the west coast of British Columbia. Bob started to chuckle, which I thought a bit odd.

"It's in Caraquet, New Brunswick, on the east coast. It's the *Fort Ross* an old Hudson's Bay ship that has been used as a herring packer for the last few years." Hardly believing what I was hearing I asked:

"Does that mean..." Bob cut me off:

"Yep, we'll have to bring her back through the Carribean and the Panama Canal."

"Does that mean..." I started to say and Bob cut me off again.
"Yep, we'll have to do our diving in the

warm, clear, waters of the Carribean, rather than the cold waters of the west coast of Vancouver Island. Think you guys can handle that?"

"Oh, hell, everyone will be disappointed, but I'll try to convince them!"

Bob laughed and hung up.

A "dream dive" suddenly changed

Needless to say my thoughts of the west coast of Vancouver Island as being the "dream dive" quickly changed. That phone call had suddenly expanded my thinking. As I talked with other members of the dive group, their thinking expanded as well.

That call started an adventure that will be recounted later in this book.

I now want to "fast forward" to the year 2000. I was writing **The Warm Dry Boat**, a book on how to keep a boat warm and dry in cooler climates, or cool and dry in warmer ones, when I heard about three adventurers from Nanaimo, British Columbia, who had made it through the Northwest Passage in a single season.

They did so in a 27' steel motor sailer built by one of them. They became only the fourth private vessel in history to accomplish that feat and only the 60th vessel of any kind to do so. The reason I chased down one of the crew was to gather some information on a small wood burning stove they used on the trip.

I got the information from George Hone, the first mate on the trip. During my phone conversations with him he told me he had about 50,000 words about the trip on a computer disk but didn't know where to go from there. Fur-

ther discussions ensued and the upshot was I ended up editing and publishing his book, **The Northwest Passage On Ten Dollars A Day**. In case you think that story was thrown in only as a plug for George's book, you're wrong. Well, mostly wrong.

As I was doing additional research for George's book he brought me a small 43 page booklet entitled **The North-West Passage, 1940-1942 and 1944.** The book chronicles the saga of the *St. Roch*, the famous Royal Canadian Mounted Police schooner, during its two way trip through the Passage. It was written by Sgt. Henry Larsen, the *St. Roch's* skipper for most of the vessel's active service life.

As I read through Sgt. Larsen's account of the return trip, westward from Halifax to Vancouver in 1944, I came across his account of his "almost meeting" with the Hudson's Bay Company ship *Fort Ross*. From that account it appears that the *Fort Ross* was far more famous than any of us realized in 1969 as we put our adventure together.

It also appears, from Sgt. Larsen's little book, that *Fort Ross* might well have set a record that has, for decades, been attributed to the *St. Roch*.

I'll get back to that record later.

When *Fort Ross* completed her trip to Vancouver she began a varied career ranging from carrying timber cruisers and tree planters, in British Columbia, to shark fishing off the west coast of Central America.

Fort Ross lost to the Contras

Unfortunately the Fort Ross became a little

known victim of U.S. President Ronald Reagan's scheme to circumvent the U.S. Congress in what became known as the Iran Contra scandal. The U.S. administration was funding an anti communist uprising in Nicaragua in an attempt to overthrow the then pro communist central government. The rebels were known as the Contras, The U.S. Congress cut off that funding, so Reagan sold arms to Iran and used the proceeds to, surreptitiously continue funding the Contras. Bob and his wife Bev abandoned the vessel two hours before the Contra firing squad showed up and escaped back to Canada. The *Fort Ross* was lost to the rebels and reportedly sank.

It is not the intention of this book in any way to lessen the accomplishments of the *St. Roch*, which were truly historically significant. The service of the RCMP ship has been chronicled in print and on film and television, most of it focusing on her trips through the Northwest Passage, 1940-42 from west to east, and 1944 from east to west. However if one looks at printed history one would almost think that the *St. Roch* was the only ship that accomplished anything in the Arctic. Nothing could be further from the truth.

A purpose of this book other than to chronicle our trip is to try to bring some balance into the discussion of Arctic exploration and some knowledge of at least one of the other ships that slugged it out day after grinding day in freezing water, penetrating cold, and tough, grinding ice.

It should be noted neither Sgt. Larsen himself, nor the RCMP as an institution, ever claimed that the *St. Roch* was anything other than a floating police detachment bringing law and order to Canada's Arctic and asserting Canadian sovereignty over the area.

It should also be noted that Sgt. Larsen never claimed the *St. Roch* was the first vessel to circumnavigate North America. In fact his own writing seems to indicate that was not the case.

The writer has referred to Larsen by the rank he held, Sergeant, when he was the "commander," as he put it, of the *St. Roch*. In fact, Sgt. Larsen was promoted to Inspector shortly after completing the east to west passage in 1944, but not because he had done the trips or set any records. His promotion was based on his time in service and the fact that he had carried out his assignment as an RCMP officer in a professional and competent manner. In 1953 Larsen was again promoted, this time to Superintendent, the rank he held when he retired from the RCMP in 1961.

The Hudson's Bay Company

It is not possible to have a balanced record of any type of Arctic exploration, business or development without at least a cursory discussion of the role of the Hudson's Bay Company, or The Bay, as it is now known.

This company, incorporated May 2, 1670, is the oldest continuous operating company in the world. In 1668, two years before its formal incorporation, its ships, starting with a 53' (16 meter) square rigged trading ketch, *Nonsuch*, were actively exploring Hudson Bay, opening trade with the local aboriginal inhabitants of the area. *Nonsuch* had spent four months battling through the North Atlantic to Hudson Bay.

This is the ex-lawyer coming out, but I am

not, nor have I ever been, an employee or a manager of The Bay nor have I ever owned, legally or beneficially, shares in the company. The Bay has not, in any way, contributed to the writing or the publication of this book. This book, therefore, is based on my own research and opinions and any mistakes are mine, are honest ones, and are not motivated by outside consideration.

This book will not be one of those dry historical painfully detailed treatises, suitable for only those who like historical facts and figures. Hopefully our story of bringing the *Fort Ross* from the east to the west coast will prove interesting, amusing and perhaps even helpful for those planning to do some long range cruising.

Since this book is about a ship as well as our trip, there will be a fair amount of discussion on getting the ship ready and how she handled the trip. In other words even the sections dealing with the trip will contain more about the ship than the usual "travel" things one reads. Hopefully this will bring a balance to the adventure that readers, especially serious boaters, will find informative as well as interesting.

Of course the danger in this approach is that it will end up satisfying neither the armchair sailor nor the blue water boater. Oh well! The problem with writing a book that involves history, particularly the history of a vessel, is that history keeps changing as more information is unearthed.

As noted when we decided to help bring the *Fort Ross* around from the east coast to Van-

couver no one had any idea about the vessel or her history other than the fact the *Fort Ross* had been built for the Hudson's Bay Company and for the two years before we brought her to Vancouver she had been used as a herring packer.

It wasn't until this book was started about three decades after our trip that some historical research came into play. My research, as a lawyer, was limited to legal research and that was about it.

So when I wrote this book the "research " that I did would be better described as something I "stumbled into."

That included Henry Larsen's booklet referred to elsewhere in this book. Larsen's wording in that little booklet has opened up the possibility it was the *Fort Ross*, and not the *St. Roch* that was the first vessel to circumnavigate North America.

I stumbled across that booklet as I was editing George Hone's book, **The Northwest Passage On Ten Dollars a Day**. It was tossed in with a pile of other printed material George had accumulated during the voyage through the passage.

The historic photographs that appeared in the first printings of this book came from various fisheries museums and the Hudson's Bay Company archives in Winnipeg. I stumbled onto one of the small maritime museums and staff there pointed me to the archives.

Section 1

Hudson's Bay Company
Some Early History

No study of the far north is complete without an examination of the Hudson's Bay Company, probably the single most significant organization in the development of the Arctic.

This company was incorporated in England May 2, 1670, making it the oldest continuous corporate entity in the world. It was incorporated by a Royal Charter of King Charles II of England and the original name was a mouthful, "The Governor and Company of Adventurers tradeing into Hudson's Bay." The company was authorized by its Charter to be "Lordes and Proprietors of Rupert's Land."

"Rupert's Land" was further defined as all the land drained by rivers flowing into Hudson Bay. In 1670 they did not know it, but the "Adventurers" took over a territory covering about 40 percent of modern Canada, plus parts of Minnesota and North Dakota. Its boundaries were what is now Quebec, in the east, Alberta in the west, the Arctic in the north, and into the United States in the south.

The Charter authorized the Adventurers to build forts, raise armies, wage wars, found colonies, enforce laws and drive out competitors. A modern corporate president would give his or her right arm to have powers like that! In fact the powers of many modern heads of state are not so broad or sweeping. At the time of its creation the "Company of Adventurers" controlled territory larger than all of Europe.

This British company, strangely, was set in motion by the early explorations of two Frenchmen, Radisson and Groseilliers, who, in about 1661, pushed westward into Canada, just north of Lake Superior.

In their discussions with local aboriginals, Cree and Ojibway, the two Frenchmen were told that constant war between two other aboriginal tribes, the Huron and the Iroquois, had disrupted the traditional trade routes so that almost no trade was possible. The Cree and Ojibway wanted to trade furs for items brought from the communities settled by Europeans in eastern Canada.

The aboriginals told the two explorers that they would happily trade with them if a trade route could be found that avoided the episodic, ongoing war and slaughter to the south. Radisson and Groseilliers returned to Montreal, their trading headquarters, suggesting the development of a trade route north, into Hudson Bay.

The trade barons in Montreal, then a colony of France, as was most of what is now eastern Canada, showed no interest in developing such a route since fur trading was Montreal's biggest industry, and they weren't about to assist in setting up a competitive trading system.

So the two French explorers went to England in 1665 and convinced some London investors and merchants to finance a trading expedition into Hudson Bay, which had been claimed for England by Henry Hudson in 1610. That led to the 1668 *Nonsuch* expedition.

In September the *Nonsuch* skipper, Zachariah Gillam, beached his little ship at the mouth of the Rupert River, in James Bay, and built a shelter to protect his trade goods and his 10 man crew from the harshness and icy cold of the coming winter.

Spring brought trade

In the spring aboriginal traders, Crees in that area, brought the furs they had trapped during the winter and, after the usual formalities of gift exchanges, a trading arrangement was made. By mid June the little ship's hold was crammed with valuable pelts; beaver muskrat, bear, marten, lynx, fox, otter, wolf and wolverine. The Cree traders returned inland with their knives, files, needles, beads, hoop iron, blankets, kettles, hatchets and other European goods. The *Nonsuch* left for London.

To say that the backers of the expedition were happy when the ship docked was an understatement. Those backers included some of Europe's most influential and powerful bankers, ship owners and merchants. The English king himself, Charles II, had an interest in the initial expedition.

The fact that the explorers had, in one trip, forged a potentially highly profitable bond between traders living in northern Canada and the powerful commercial establishment in Europe, was not lost on the Europeans. That one trip had focused the fur trade northward, into Hudson Bay and away from Montreal, avoiding both the wars to the south and the politics and machinations of the Montreal business and political community. Thus the Chartering of the "Company of Adventurers."

Soon after the corporate organization of the company more ships were sent to Hudson Bay and a trading pattern similar to that set up by the *Nonsuch* continued for more than two centuries.

The company set up permanent trading posts at the mouths of all the rivers flowing into Hudson and James Bay. These posts were the first permanent communities in the North. Company traders built alliances with the various aboriginal tribes, Cree, Ojibwa, Montagnais and Assiniboine. As the word of the availability of trade goods at the Hudson's Bay trading posts spread west, trade expanded and flourished.

Expanded operations

From 1670, the date of their incorporation, until 1869, 199 years, the "Adventurers" pushed the frontiers of the company's operations to the high Arctic, the Pacific Coast of what is now Canada and down the west coast of what is now the United States to south of the Columbia River.

On the west coast the Hudson's Bay Company set up Fort Vancouver, now Vancouver, Washington in 1825. That city, located on the north side of the Columbia River opposite Portland,

Hudson's Bay Arctic post building at Fort Leopold. Photograph courtesy of Ken Burton.

Oregon, is the oldest town in Washington State. The other Vancouver on the west coast, Vancouver, British Columbia did not become a city for another 50 years.

John McLoughlin with his assistant, James Douglas, ran the Bay's west coast empire, very profitably, from Fort Vancouver for more than 20 years. In 1846, after the final settlement of the western Canada /US border dispute, which set the international boundary at the 49th parallel, the Bay moved its western operation to Fort Victoria, on Vancouver Island.

The HBC site at Vancouver, Washington, has been reconstructed as it existed during the 1830's and 1840's, and is now part of a 370 acre National Historic Reserve.

In 1858 James Douglas became the first Governor of British Columbia.

The "Baymen" as they came to be known did serious battle, both commercially and physically, with their competitors, The Northwest Company, commonly known as the "Montrealers.". As time went on, and the population grew, fur trading became of lesser importance as the company became a general retailer - one business among many other businesses in the growing settlements.

"Baymen" and "Montrealers" merge

The competition with the Northwest Company was resolved in an age old business manner. The two companies merged and once again the monopoly was restored.

The "merger" became, in effect, a takeover by the Baymen. With the monopoly restored the Baymen, as those holding monopolies often do, became arrogant and high handed. It appeared to many that profit became the only driving force. To say this attitude upset local settlers was an understatement.

Canada, as a country, came into existence in 1867 and one of the first items on the new government's agenda was to abolish what one of the fathers of confederation called "the injurious and demoralizing sway of the Hudson's Bay Company."

Within two years the company had, in negotiations with the Canadian and British governments, negotiated away all of it's right, title and interest in its original charter and had become a commercial enterprise, much the same as other commercial enterprises of the era. The lands covered by the charter were incorporated into what is now Canada. The company as part of the negotiated settlement received 7,000,000 acres of land.

200 years of building

In the almost 200 years the Company had been operating it had built up a substantial infrastructure of forts, lines of communication and trading posts all across Canada and in the northern United States, particularly in what is now the U.S. Pacific Northwest. It was, therefore, well positioned to become a major retailer throughout the country. It did exactly that. The trading posts became "general" retail stores but did not give up on the fur trade.

With the development of the company as a general retailer the requirement for transport increased dramatically. It was one thing to,

once a year, transport a handful of trading goods to a remote Arctic post and return with a load of pelts. It was quite another thing to haul general merchandise to supply many retail outlets. The Bay, therefore, continued it's shipbuilding program, and in 1938 the *Fort Ross* was built. It was one of the 184 ships that have flown the Hudson's Bay Company flag since that first 53 footer, *Nonsuch*, bashed it's way into Hudson Bay in 1668. That number, 184, does not included the thousands of smaller boats, canoes and barges, many of them up to 40' long, that shuttled Bay goods along the inland rivers and lakes.

HBC and Arctic exploration

The role of the Hudson's Bay Company in early Arctic exploration is not as well known as it's role in the development of the North American fur trade, in its earliest days, and general retailing in its later years. As the world's oldest continuing corporate entity that is not surprising. The fact that HBC employees generally did not see the tasks they performed, on a day to day basis, in any historical context at the time they were performing them, meant that they didn't always record what they did. It is only in the context of later research that what was done by HBC employees, actively supported, and in some cases mandated, by the company, comes into historical focus.

In fact it was an Hudon's Bay Company employee, John Rae, who solved two of the world's most puzzling riddles of the mid 1800s. These were the fate of the 1845 Sir John Franklin expedition and the location of the final link of the Northwest Passage. Until relatively recently the general public knew little of the role of either Rae or the HBC in connection with either event.

Franklin's last expedition

Franklin's expedition left England in May of 1845, one of many that, over the years, had been sent out to discover the Northwest Passage. It was a state of the art expedition and the most expensive launched to that time. Its two ships, *Erebus* and *Terror*, were specially reinforced to battle the ice and boasted 20 horsepower steam engines, complete with retractable screw propellers. The ships were equipped with hot water heating systems, early cameras, a library containing more than 1,000 volumes, hand organs and enough supplies to last three years.

In July, while he waited at the entrance of Lancaster Sound for the ice to clear, Franklin met two whaling ships. After leaving them he was never seen or heard from again.

Aircraft and Fort Ross *in winter cover. These aircraft established Canadian sovereignty in the air over all of the Arctic.*

John Rae was born in 1813 on the Orkney Islands, located off the north coast of Scotland almost due east of the southern tip of Greenland and the entrance to Davis Strait.

Early explorers, in the days before instruments for ascertaining longitude, could simply sail due west from the natural harbor at Stromness, on the west side of the Islands, to Greenland and North America. Stromness also had fine fresh water at Login's Well. Almost all early travelers, the Vikings, Martin Frobisher, James Cook, Edwin Parry, Henry Hudson, and the fur trading ships of the HBC, stopped at Stromness for fresh water and other provisions.

HBC hiring Orcadians

When HBC ships stopped at Stromness they quickly noticed that the local residents were well educated, hardy and industrious. They also noted that they were excellent fishermen and boat handlers. Most of them, unlike their counterparts from England and other parts of Scotland, could read and write and so made good record keepers. This accounts for the fact that most of the HBC trading post managers had Scottish names, something that often puzzles the casual reader or historian.

Between 1772 and 1800 the HBC expanded its work force from 180 to 600 and 75 percent of the employees were from the Orkneys.

In 1833 John Rae, a medical doctor by education, became one of those HBC employees. He signed on as the doctor on the *Prince of Wales*, a ship heading for Rupert's Land, the domain of the HBC.

He was following in the footsteps of his two older brothers who had earlier sailed away with the HBC. In fact, since 1819 Rae's father had been the HBC representative in the Islands.

Rae liked it so well he stayed on

Young Rae enjoyed his first voyage so much that he spent the next 23 years in HBC service retiring in 1856. He became the ultimate Arctic explorer, surveyor and traveler.

A new book, **Fatal Passage**, by Ken McGoogan, published in 2001, by Harper Flamingo Canada, gives a brilliantly researched, detailed and well written account of the Arctic endeavors of John Rae and finally sets the record straight about probably the foremost explorers of the Canadian Arctic.

McGoogan's book also finally gives the Hudson's Bay Company the credit it deserves for the serious geographical, surveying and map making work it commissioned during the early days of Arctic exploration. In the search for the Franklin expedition many HBC employees, other than Rae, spent months beating through the Arctic, without success.

In 1854 John Rae, with a small party of seasoned men, set out to survey and map the remaining unmapped section of the northern coast of North America. The maps of the time, done by various other explorers, showed King William Island as a peninsula named King William Land.

As Rae pressed north, along the west coast of the Boothia Peninsula, the charts showed that the coast line should be turning west. It was not. On May 6, 1854, he stood on a point of land he named Point de la Guiche, and looked out over a frozen channel where the naval charts of the time showed there should be land. Rae also noted that the ice he was looking at was "young ice" not the rougher, older ice he had encountered in his previous explorations on the west side of what was then known as King William Land.

"Land" was really an "Island"

Rae correctly concluded that King William Land was, in fact, an island. It protected the channel he was looking at from the grinding, ship smashing, impenetrable pack ice that flowed down Victoria Straight, on the west side of King William Island.

Rae had, in fact, discovered the final link in the Northwest Passage, but it was not for another half century, until the 1903-1906 voyage of

Roald Amundsen, that the route was finally traversed.

The weather conditions, distances involved, the coming spring thawand the condition of his men caused Rae to conclude that he could not finish his survey without risking lives so he turned back and after an 11day trek reached the snow huts of Pelly Bay. There he bought, from a local Inuit, a silver fork and spoon with the initials "F.R.M.C." scratched onto them with some sharp object.

Rae briefly thought about the lost Franklin expedition, but conventional wisdom at the time was that Franklin had been lost much further north. He speculated that the utensils had belonged to other lost European vessels.

Franklin's fate determined

Rae continued south and arrived, 20 days later, at Repulse Bay. There he found the three men he had left at the "base" camp some months before had struck up a relationship with local Inuit who also had items to sell. Rae bought all of them, pieces of watches, compasses, telescopes and guns. He also bought several sterling silver spoons and forks bearing Franklin's crest and a small silver plate engraved "Sir John Franklin, K.C.H."

Rae spent days interviewing the Inuit. In 1851 Inuit had found about 30 bodies near Ogle Point. It was also clear from the items Rae had purchased that he had discovered the fate of the Franklin expedition. Worse than that, from the Inuit reports of the state of the bodies and the content of the cooking kettles, Rae concluded the men had resorted to cannibalism.

Rae's report "leaked"

Rae dutifully reported his findings to his superiors who forwarded them to the Admiralty in London. Rae himself left for London soon after finishing his discussions with the Inuit. When Rae arrived in London he found that his confidential report to his superiors, complete with the comment on cannibalism, had been "leaked" to the newspapers and Victorian England was revulsed by the news.

More important, Lady Franklin, the wife of Sir John, concerned about her husband's, and her own, place in history was so upset with Rae that she spent the rest of her life attacking him. She seems to have adopted the position that if you don't like the message, you (figuratively, of course) shoot the messenger. With her political and social connections, and her money, she almost succeeded. Franklin is widely credited with "discovering" the Northwest Passage, when, in fact, all he did was wreck his state of the art ships and get his crew killed. In retrospect he was a disaster.

However Lady Franklin was able to enlist the aid of the politically and socially powerful, as well as other explorers jealous of Rae's success. It is interesting to note that Rae is the only major Arctic figure of the time that never received a knighthood, despite the fact that he accomplished far more than most.

The Hudson's Bay Company not only paid Rae as its employee but also funded all the expeditions he put together during his 23 years with the Company. The HBC was, in fact, one of the major funders of serious geographical, survey and exploration work in the Arctic.

Fort Ross *iced in on Chaleur Bay*

Section 2

Fort Ross Construction Details

When building ships for Arctic service early builders were limited to the traditional boat building material - wood. Even after iron and steel became available, many owners continued building in wood for two reasons. The first was that they knew the material and trusted it and the second was that for vessels required to winter frozen into Arctic ice, wood was self insulating. The *Fort Ross* was no exception.

However those used to seeing wooden boats built for normal service are often amazed at the size of the components used in Arctic ships. The *Fort Ross* was typical of such ships.

Fort Ross was designed by W.J. Roue of Halifax, Nova Scotia, a designer who, in 1921, designed one of the most famous schooners the world has ever seen, the *Bluenose*. For decades, a likeness of *Bluenose* has been embossed on the reverse of the Canadian dime.

W.J Roue (1879-1970) became one of the most famous marine designers in the world, not only for the speed of his sail designs but because of how he arrived at those designs. He was the first Canadian marine designer, and among the first in the world, who actually "designed" a ship on paper, and produced a set of blueprints from which a ship was built. Prior to that time ships were built using a scale half model of the hull. The hull shape was usually developed by the builders.

Roue began making his own toy boats when he was four years old. A year later he took one of his sailing models to his father and asked him to fix some lead ballast outside the hull. Even at five years Roue was way ahead of his time. Almost no one was using exterior ballast at that time. By the time he was 13 he was designing and building five foot sailing models that two men, rowing a light skiff, could not catch.

Roue read everything he could on the subject of naval architecture. He haunted the docks and the Royal Nova Scotia Yacht Squadron. A member of the Yacht Squadron gave him a copy of Dixon-Kemp's Yachting Architecture, the yacht design bible at the time. Roue literally wore it out and ended up memorizing almost all of it.

As was normal at the time, Roue left school at the age of 16. He took a job as a clerk with a grocery wholesaler and studied mechanical

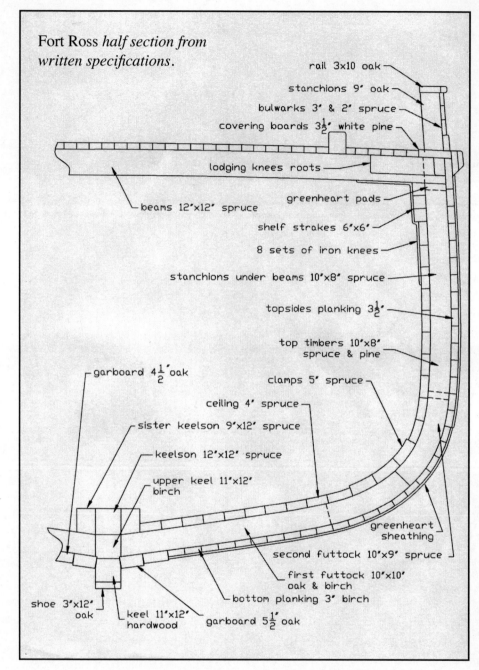

Fort Ross *half section from written specifications*.

rail 3x10 oak

stanchions 9" oak

bulwarks 3" & 2" spruce

covering boards 3½" white pine

lodging knees roots

greenheart pads

beams 12"x12" spruce

shelf strakes 6"x6"

8 sets of iron knees

stanchions under beams 10"x8" spruce

topsides planking 3½"

top timbers 10"x8" spruce & pine

garboard 4½" oak

clamps 5" spruce

ceiling 4" spruce

sister keelson 9"x12" spruce

keelson 12"x12" spruce

upper keel 11"x12" birch

greenheart sheathing

second futtock 10"x9" spruce

first futtock 10"x10" oak & birch

bottom planking 3" birch

shoe 3"x12" oak

keel 11"x12" hardwood

garboard 5½" oak

and bottling plant and, at age 24, Roue went into the family business.

He worked diligently and effectively but, on his own time, he pursued his passion, marine design. His break came in 1907 when he designed a yacht for the vice commodore of the Yacht Squadron. During the next 11 years, while continuing to work full time at the bottling plant, Roue designed 14 more vessels.

In late 1920 Roue was approached to design a working vessel capable of operating as a fishing vessel, but also capable of recapturing the International Fishermen's Trophy that had been lost to the American fleet in Gloucester, Massachusetts. The Trophy was awarded to the fastest working

drafting at night. He entered yacht design competitions run by various yachting publications, particularly Rudder magazine. In one competition he won an honorable mention.

His father owned a soft drink manufacturing

fishing vessel in a competition between a U.S. vessel out of Gloucester and a Canadian vessel out of Lunenburg, N.S.

The resulting design was named *Bluenose* and the rest is history. Despite the success of his design, Roue did not become a full time marine designer until 1934!

How well designed and how fast?

Just how well designed and how fast was Bluenose? Joan Roue, Roue's great grand daughter, in her book, **A Spirit Deep Within**, recounts the story of a Canadian naval officer on the destroyer *Champlain*. In 1930 *Champlain* was accompanying *Bluenose* to a race in Gloucester and Hugh F. Pullen, a Canadian Navy Rear Admiral (Retired), said his ship had to do:

"14 knots just to keep up with her."

His destroyer had to go full out just to keep up with *Bluenose* and *Bluenose* was just cruising along!

In examining Roue's designs it is clear he followed the school of design that dictated a good marine designer must be 75% artist and 25% engineer. His designs, even for work boats, and that included *Bluenose* and *Fort Ross* are considered by many to be works of art.

With her design done by the country's foremost marine designer it is little wonder that *Fort Ross* is considered by many to be one of the most "eye pleasing" designs ever produced for what was, in effect, a small freighter. Yet she had all of the strength and structural integrity needed to operate for years in the Arctic, probably the harshest marine environment in the world.

Fort Ross was built in 1938 by H. Melbourne Leary of Dayspring, Nova Scotia and J.A. Weingart, of Shelburne, Nova Scotia, at the Leary brother's shipyard in Dayspring. The yard was located on the LaHave River, 12 miles inland

from the Atlantic Ocean. Ships have been built at the Leary yard since 1876. The yard continues in existence today as Snyder's Shipyard Ltd., having been purchased from the Leary brothers in 1944 by Reginald "Teddy" Snyder. Snyder was the foreman of the 39 man crew that built the *Fort Ross*.

After her launching *Fort Ross* was towed to Lunenburg Foundry Co. for the installation of her engine and other machinery. She underwent machinery trials June 16, 1938, and her 240 HP, six cylinder Canadian Fairbanks Morse direct reversing diesel engine drove her at 8.75 knots.

The engine had a 10" bore, a 12.5" stroke and top RMP was 400. It was two cycle, fresh water cooled and was equipped with a air start system. The basic measurements of the *Fort Ross* were:

Length - overall	127' 0"
Beam	28' 5"
Molded depth	14' 4"
Draft - light	Fore: 5' 4"
	Aft: 8' 10"
Draft - loaded	Fore: 10'6"
	Aft: 12' 0"
Deadweight Tonnage	275 - including fuel

Frames were specified to be 10" x 10" on 18" centers. This means that there was only 8", less than a normal man's hand span, between them. However, even the specifications don't tell the whole story of the vessel's great strength. As noted in the photo, each frame had a "sister" frame bolted along side likely at the place where the main frame pieces were scarfed together. This reduced the spacing between the frames to less than six inches.

Fort Ross *in frame. Photo: Hudson's Bay Archives, Provincial Archives of Manitoba.*

Floors and deck beams were the same size on the same centers. Her keel assembly, including upper keel, keel and keelson measured 12" wide and 30" thick. In addition there was a 3" thick oak shoe on the keel and a greenheart rider. The two sister keelsons were each 9" x 12". The stern and rudder posts were 12" x 14" and her stem timber was 12" x 14". *Fort Ross* clamps were 15" thick. Her garboard planks, two on each side, were 51/2" and 41/2" inches thick, with the first being bolted to the keel with 7/8" bolts and the second bolted with 3/4" bolts. Bottom and side planking was 31/2" thick and deck planking was 3" thick. The shaft log timber measured 17" x 17".

Sheathed with Greenheart

The vessel was sheathed with greenheart and the stem and bow were protected with a spe-

cially designed 5/8" steel plate. Both these specifications recognized that *Fort Ross* would see service in the arctic ice. The vessel also had eight sets of iron knees bolted through ceiling and timbers and clenched at both ends.

The vessel hull was also planked inside with 3" planking. Insulation of the cabin spaces was rock wool between wall studs. All frames were creosoted under ceiling and planking

The 6,500 imperial gallons of diesel fuel was carried in three steel tanks, as was 200 gallons of lubricating oil. Two fresh water tanks held 750 gallons each. The vessel was equipped with a 200 gallon sewage holding tank, complete with pump.

Fort Ross had two masts, 18" in diameter at the deck and, while the original specs called for her to be rigged as a schooner with three sails, a fore staysail, fore trysail and main trysail, it appears that, in fact, the vessel was never rigged. The crows nest, or "ice bucket", as it was sometimes called, was fitted to the foremast and measured 3' x 4' x 6' and was accessed by a ladder on each side. The standing rigging was to be "best galvanized iron rope..." Galvanized fastenings were specified throughout the vessel.

56" x 36" wheel and 41/2" shaft

The ship was propelled by a 56" x 36" three bladed propellor attached to a 4.5" diameter steel tail shaft, fitted with a continuous brass liner. She carried a spare tail shaft. Air for engine starting was provided by two air compressors, one driven by the main engine and the other driven independently. The independent unit produced 10 cubic feet per minute at a pressure of 250 pounds per square inch.

Fort Ross steering gear was chain and cable with leads and quarter blocks to the steering quadrant. The main helm wheel was located in the pilot house with a second helm station on top of the pilot house, geared to the pilot house wheel. Wheel house communications with the engine room were via both a telegraph and a speaking tube.

The vessel specifications called for four stoves, three capable of burning either wood or coal and the other burning diesel. The galley stove was large, with a 28"x35.5" top. The mess room stove was slightly smaller as was the pilot house stove. The engine room had a diesel stove.

Fort Ross *inside framing. Photo: Hudson's Bay Archives, Provincial Archives of Manitoba.*

A salty ship

Specifications called for *Fort Ross* to be salted. The reason for salting a vessel is based on the fact that only fresh water will cause wood to develop rot, and therefore, dry rot when the rotting wood dries. Salt water, in effect, pickles the wood and helps prevent rot from starting. Salted vessels had additional time added to their seaworthiness certificate and therefore had to be inspected less often. When a vessel was salted any fresh water dripping into the vessel mixed with the salt, creating salt water that helped retard rotting.

The salting process itself was relatively simple. During construction the spaces between the frames, except in the bilges, were filled with salt. The keelson was encased in wood and salt packed into the space between the casing and the keelson.

The planking on the inside of the frames held the salt in place and a horizontal plank between the frames and the interior planking and the hull kept the whole mess from sliding into the bilge. Salting was not required in the bilge area since water entering the bilge through the shaft log, or seeping in through planking seams, was sea water.

To further protect the wooden vessel from rotting, all frames were creosoted before ceilings

Fort Ross looking aft. *Photo: Fisheries Museum of the Atlantic.*

Fort Ross *looking aft. Photo: Fisheries Museum of the Atlantic.*

or planking was added. Before the Greenheart sheathing was installed burlap was tacked to the hull planking and coated with a mixture of Stockholm tar and pitch. Stockholm tar was a very sticky paste made from the resinous saps of pinewoods.

Various woods

The vessel was built with various species of wood. When examining and comparing woods it is useful to keep in mind that, generally speaking, lighter weight woods are very soft and heavier weight woods are very hard. Balsa wood weighs eight pounds per cubic foot. It

is considered to be a very soft, weak wood. Ligum vitae, on the other hand, weighing 80 pounds per cubic foot, is considered a very hard wood.

Birch was specified for the upper keel, stem, apron, stern post, first buttock, bilge and bottom planking, and engine beds. Birch weighs 40-45 pounds per cubic foot, is a hard wood and has a very high resistance to splitting. Oak weighs in at about 45 pounds per cubic foot and was specified for the keel shoe, first futtock (along with birch), stanchions, rails, garboard planks, bow chocks, hatch coamings

Fort Ross *close to launching. Photo: Fisheries Museum of the Atlantic.*

and shaft log. *Fort Ross* floors were specified to be at least 80% oak. Oak is a hard wood and has a good resistance to splitting.

Spruce was specified for the second futtock, top timber (along with pine) keelson, sister keelson, hook and pointers, ceiling, between bilge and clamps, clamps, stanchions under beams and hatches, beams, shelf strakes, bulwarks, masts, derricks and waterways. Spruce weighs about 28 pounds per cubic foot, is considered a wood of medium hardness and has good torsional strength and split resistance. This type of spruce, white spruce, (also sometimes call eastern spruce) should not be confused with sitka spruce, (sometimes called western spruce) which is softer, lighter and not as strong.

White pine was specified for deck planking and covering boards. White pine weighs about 25 pounds per cubic foot, is very soft and has a poor resistance to splitting.

To help in comparing the wood used in the construction of *Fort Ross*, teak (Burmese) weighs 45 pounds per cubic foot, is a hard wood with high split resistance. Douglas fir weighs 35 pounds per cubic foot, is medium hard with a fair split resistance.

Section 3

The Arctic

Whenever a potential owner approaches a designer to design a vessel, the first thing a good designer asks is something along the lines of "what are you going to do with this boat?" The prospective owner usually then tells the designer where the vessel will operate and what he will want the vessel to be able to do. In the case of the *Fort Ross* the area of operations was to be the Arctic and it was to be a small freighter, capable of surviving in one of the most dangerous and harshest marine environments on the planet.

The Arctic is generally described as that area north of 66 degrees 32 minutes latitude, a line commonly known as the Arctic Circle. It is an area of approximately eight million square miles and contains a variety of climates and vegetation. In the southern portion are the northern sections of the taiga, the forests of spruce, poplar, birch and fir that carpet the temperate northern climates around the world. To the north of the taiga there is the tundra, a relatively flat, plain-like area where the main vegetation is moss, lichens and various swamps and swamp grasses. Generally the subsoil on the tundra, that soil just a few inches below the surface, is frozen year round.

To the north of the tundra is what is known to some as the High Arctic where ice perpetually covers some of the land and most of the four million square miles of the Arctic Ocean. The ice advances and retreats depending on the season and global climatic conditions. As George Hone, author of **The Northwest Passage On Ten Dollars A Day**, one of the most recent works on the transit of the Northwest Passage by a small vessel, says:

"There are 'good' ice years and 'bad' ice years. In a good ice year it is possible for a small boat, with an experienced crew, to safely transit the Passage. In a bad ice year even the most powerful ships, ice-reinforced, can't go anywhere."

The Northwest Passage is generally described as a sea passage across the North American continent, through the Canadian Arctic from the Atlantic to the Pacific oceans. It is generally considered that a vessel has completed a transit of the Passage when it has crossed the Arctic Circle heading north in one of the oceans and recrossed the Arctic Circle heading south in the other.

Manhattan *getting ready.*

sage ice and commercially transport oil from the fields of Prudhoe Bay on Alaska's north slope to the South 48. The ship, with its 43,000 horsepower turbine engines, armored steel ice blister, and three acre deck, was stopped cold by the arctic ice and had to call upon the Canadian ice breaker *John A. Macdonald* to free her .

In fact the *Manhattan* had two ice breakers along to assist. The Johnny Mac, as the *John A. Macdonald* came to be called by those on the trip and the *Northwind*, a U.S. ice breaker. *Northwind* had to return to Seattle, its home base, before the trip concluded.

Manhattan had tried to take the northern route through the passage, through M'Clure Strait, but even with ice breaker support, it couldn't make it. It had to take the more normal southern route. Using that route *Manhattan* made it through the ice, but its backers came to the conclusion that transiting oil by tanker through the Northwest Passage was not economically feasible.

Clearly, 1968 was not a good "ice year."

If one could spread the ice found in both the Arctic and Antarctic over the entire world, like butter on toast, Dr. Charles Swithinbank of the Scott Polar Institute estimated in 1968, it would be 600 feet deep. Dr. Swithinbank's comments can be found in a 1970 book entitled **The Northwest Passage From the Mathew to the Manhattan: 1497 to 1969.**

Types of ice

Inuit have about 100 words in their language to describe various types of ice they have faced over the centuries they have inhabited the arc-

In 1968 the 1,005', 150,000 ton tanker *Manhattan* underwent a $36,000,000 refit, turning her into the world's largest ice breaker. Manhattan was to test the theory that such a ship could bash its way through the Northwest Pastic. Modern sailors are most concerned about the extent of ice cover and the hardness of ice. The reason for concerns about the extent of ice cover is self evident. No ice means clear and easy sailing. New ice - ice that has formed in the current year - is generally "soft" and that means relatively easy sailing as long as the ships are reasonably reinforced. It also means that ice breaker support is generally not required.

Multi year ice - ice that has been forming over the years without intermittently melting - is as hard as granite. This is the type of ice that causes even experienced ice breaker captains to shudder. This is also the type of ice that stopped the *Manhattan*, with all her power and ice reinforcing, in her attempt to transit M'Clure Strait. In the end it was this type of ice that convinced shipping experts that there was no economically feasible way to bring Alaskan oil south by tanker. Thus the Alaska pipe line was built.

Weather conditions

Operating in ice was not the only hardship facing the *Fort Ross* and her HBC crew during her Arctic operations. There was also the weather.

The Arctic is not, contrary to popular opinion, the coldest place on earth. Temperatures in Siberia, and the Yukon and Tanana river valleys of the Canadian Yukon Territory are often up to 20F (12C) degrees colder than along the Northwest Passage. In fact places in Alaska, North Dakota, Wyoming and Montana, along with areas in Northern Ontario and Quebec, regularly register temperatures colder than the Arctic.

While the fact that many places in North

America have a few colder days during the winter than the Arctic is interesting, it is not really significant in assessing the effect of the temperature in the Arctic. At Barrow, Alaska, the northernmost community in the U.S., there are 324 days a year when the temperature is below freezing. That means that only 41 days per year have temperatures above freezing and even during those few days, in the summer, the temperature averages only 40F (4.4C) and Barrow is towards the southern latitudes of the Arctic and the Northwest Passage.

This is the reason that no more than about four to six inches of the top soil melts during the summer. Deeper than that the earth is frozen year round.

Because of the permanently frozen ground, very few water or sewer pipes can be laid. Most houses have two tanks, one for water and another for sewage. One truck delivers water to the homes and another hauls away the sewage.

The polar desert

Precipitation in the arctic is very low, less than an average of 20 inches a year, less precipitation than in Las Vegas, Nevada. Barter Island, in the Canadian arctic, has about the same precipitation as Death Valley, the driest place in the U.S. The winds throughout the area can come up very suddenly and whip the snow into a blinding blizzard. Those winds, combined with the penetrating cold, can be deadly.

In many places in the arctic ropes are strung between buildings so that people can move safely from one site to another during blizzards. There is a story told of a group of whalers playing baseball on the frozen bay when one of these severe wind storms struck. They tried to scramble for shelter, but before they reached safety, five of them got lost and froze to death.

George Hone, in his book, **The Northwest Passage On Ten Dollars A Day**, recounts a story of a friend of his in Cambridge Bay who based his plane at the airport there. During one particularly fierce blizzard, driven by 60 mile per hour winds, one of the airport workers

Fort Ross in the ice again. *Photo: Hudson's Bay Archives, Provincial Archives of Manitoba.*

made the near fatal mistake of walking out of a hanger into the storm. Because of the driving snow he was unable to see and immediately lost his way.

Luckily for him his coworkers saw him leave, grabbed a long pole and rushed to the door.

They opened the door and flailed about with the pole "until they eventually thumped the guy," and hauled him back into the hangar. Survival is always foremost in the minds of those who operate in the arctic, even in the settled areas.

Lure of the Northwest Passage

The lure of the Northwest Passage to the very early Europeans was based on enlightened self-interest. They wanted to find a short route to the "riches of the East". Similarly modern shippers also look at the massive savings they would realize if a commercially viable sea route through the Passage was available for large cargo ships. Ships heading from Japan and Korea would have to travel up to 8,000 fewer miles if they could get to Europe through a Northwest Passage route rather than going via current routes.

Most people, when looking at one of the maps we are all used to seeing, a Mercator Projection, would think that a voyage from New York to Alaska, via Panama, is about the same distance as a trip to Alaska through the Northwest Passage. In fact the trip through the Northwest Passage is only half as far.

Some regular limited commercial use of the Northwest Passage is now being made by the Russians who are operating regular tourist trips from Russia to the United Kingdom on one of their ice breakers.

The great "disappearing ice" debate

No book that touches on topics related to the Arctic should avoid dealing, even very briefly, with the current "disappearing ice" debate. Most of the papers and articles written about the disappearing Arctic ice have adopted "the sky is falling" approach.

Supposedly intelligent scientists have theorized that when all the icebergs floating in the Arctic and Antarctic melt the ocean level will rise and flood many of our coastal cities and towns. I don't know where these guys got their science degrees, but since icebergs are already floating, and displacing their weight, when they melt there will be no appreciable change in water level! Even the most unscientific boater knows that. These same scientists have estimated that the area of Arctic ice cap has shrunk by about 43 percent.

The "sky is falling" approach has led these same scientists to conclude that global warming is the main cause of the ice melt. That, of course, has led to items like the Kyoto Accord, which would require North American industries to slash energy use by 25 percent over the next decade. Such a reduction could well result in a substantial decline in industrial output and the current North American standard of living. It is interesting to note that the Kyoto Accord is most vigorously promoted by countries that would like nothing better than to see the North American economy dragged down towards their own.

It's volume that matters

There are other scientists who have been carefully assessing the changes in the Arctic ice. They have pointed out that it is not the thickness, or the ice cover, that matters, but rather the total volume of ice. In assessing that issue these scientists point out that Arctic ice is constantly being pushed around by the Arctic winds and there is a natural fluctuation in the pattern and intensity of those winds. Sometime these winds push the ice outward from the North Pole causing it to pile up against land, mostly in the Canadian Northwest Passage. This leaves the Pole area almost ice free.

At other time the winds cause the ice to jam up at the Pole and this leave the Northwest Passage almost ice free.

In fact even the Greenpeace web site points out in 2002 that while there has been a decline of sea ice in the Barents, Kara and East Siberian seas north of Russia, there has been an increasing amount of sea ice in Davis Strait and the Labrador Sea between Canada and Greenland.

Data collected over a short time

These same scientist have concluded that there has been a normal, natural variation in the "melt season" of between 55 and 75 days from 1979 to 1996. They do note that the overall lengthening of the melt season has been about 5.3 days per decade.

They also point out that hard scientific evidence over the long term is difficult because of the relatively short time data has been collected. Some of them suggest that we may be in a normal, natural cycle that occurs over a longer time period than that for which data exists.

Fort Ross *looking aft. Photo: Fisheries Museum of the Atlantic.*

thickening. The newspaper, reporting on a paper in the Journal of Science, notes that the Ross ice streams have either slowed or stopped all together, allowing the ice to thicken.

In the same article the paper notes, based on a paper in Nature magazine, that the temperature in the Antarctic desert valleys has grown cooler by 1 F degree during the 14 year period from 1985 to 1999.

So what?

What does all of this have to do with the *Fort Ross*, ships like her, and the Hudson's Bay Company?

Let's assume that there is a global warming situation which will lead, in 30 or 40 years, to the Northwest Passage becoming navigable for at least six months of the year. That would mean that commercial shipping lanes would be available and there would be the potential for major ecological damage in the Arctic. One of the methods of reducing the likelihood of such damage would be the rules and regulation that apply to ships using that route.

It should be noted that the same "sky is falling" approach has been applied to the Antarctic where the same scientists have been trumpeting that the Antarctic ice cap is melting due to global warming.

However an article in a January 2002 issue of the Seattle Post Intelligencer, noted that, in fact, the ice cap in the Western Antarctic is

It is a well known fact that different countries have different environmental rules when it comes to shipping. Some require double hulls

Fort Ross *leaving Tuktuk August 14, 1939. Notue hailing port "Winnipeg." That was the head office of the HBC at the time. Photo: HB Archives. Provincial Archives of Manitoba.*

for oil tankers, some require holding tanks for all discharge and some even require that engine exhaust solids be screened before the exhaust can be released to the atmosphere. Some countries require that large ships have escort tugs accompany them whenever they are in that country's waters. Other countries have no meaningful regulations at all.

Flags of convenience

So who makes the rules about possible shipping in the Northwest Passage? It is commonly accepted that the Passage is in Canadian waters, at least by Canadians, so it would make sense that Canada would make the rules, right? Well that depends on who one talks to. Two of the world's most powerful maritime countries, the United States and Great Britain, have adopted the position that if a commercially viable Northwest Passage shipping lane opens up, that Passage would be an International waterway, much like the Strait of Gibralter.

That would mean the only regulations applying to ships using the Passage would be regulations in force in the country where the ships are registered and as noted earlier, there are many "flag of convenience" countries that have almost no regulations at all.

The Canadian position has been that Canada has exercised sovereignty over the area for centuries and that makes the Passage internal Canadian waters. Therefore, Canadians argue, Canada has the right, and the responsibility, to make regulations relating to the use of the waterway. In fact there are those who adopt the position that Canada could, if it chose, totally prohibit the commercial use of the waterway. The Canadian government has never adopted this latter position. The Canadian government, being typically Canadian, has not taken any really firm stand at all.

Sovereignty - what is it?

The concept of sovereignty, in its most simplistic form, and in the context of this discussion, means nothing more than that a country has control, free from outside interference, over its territory. If land is within the well defined borders of a state, no other state generally argues about it. There is no question that the U.S. has sovereignty over Death Valley or the Grand Canyon, regardless of how many people live there, or even if no one lived there.

Similarly there is no argument that Canada has sovereignty over vast, unsettled areas of the Canadian prairie.

However in areas of the world where country boundaries have not been formalized, or in the far north, where country boundaries all terminate at one point, the Geographic North Pole, there is another factor that comes into play in determining which country has sovereignty, and that is the use of the area.

And that brings us back to the *Fort Ross* and other ships like her and the Hudson's Bay Company, their owners and operators. For two centuries, from the first time the *Nonsuch* smashed its way through the ice into Hudson Bay in 1668, until "Rupert's Land" was formally turned over to the new country of Canada, in about 1868, the company operated commercially in the area on a daily basis.

HBC operated Quietly

Even after the formal turnover of its 1670 land grant, and its transition from a fur trader to a general merchandiser, the Hudson's Bay Company and its stoutly built ships operated daily in the Arctic, almost without notice as far as the rest of the world was concerned.

Great attention was heaped upon Roald Amundsen when, in about 1903, he became the first European to visit the Magnetic North Pole. Western history records him as the "first" person to accomplish that feat. The fact that local Inuit had done so 75 years earlier, and recorded the event, is almost never mentioned.

Similarly we never hear about the fact that another Hudson's Bay Company ship, the *Fort James*, was the second ship to reach that same location. The *Fort James*, built by the same yard that built the *Fort Ross*, was the second ship to reach the Magnetic North Pole but that event was but a foot note to Amundsen's exploit. As far as the skipper and crew of the *Fort James* were concerned "it was all in a day's work."

All in a day's work

"All in a day's work" is a key phrase in determining whether or not a country has established sovereignty over an area. It's one thing to pass through an area on a trip. That just makes headlines if you're the first to do it and even more headlines if you die in the process.

Operating in an area on a day to day basis, establishing settlements, business and bringing law and order, is what establishes sovereignty. The ships of the Hudson's Bay Company, including the *Fort Ross*, were instrumental in establishing Canadian claims of sovereignty over the Arctic. If the Northwest Passage ever becomes an economically viable shipping lane, and if Canada is able to successfully assert dominion over it, the country will owe a great debt to The Bay, its fleet of stout ships, like the *Fort Ross*, and the tough, iron-willed men who operated them.

Okay, so much for the history, now on to the trip.

A stop in the Arctic, at Tuktoyaktuk. Courtesy of Vancouver Maritime Museum.

Section 4

Getting Ready for the Trip

Just how does one get ready for a boat trip when the boat is on the east coast and all the crew (12 people) is on the west coast? The first, and most obvious, thing to do is to arrange a planning session. A word about planning sessions.

I am a firm believer in proper planning and, within reason, the more planning the better. Planning sessions themselves have to be properly planned. Ours usually started with the usual telephone calls, along the following lines:

"Hey, why don't we get together for a couple of beers, some food, and to do some planning." Beer is always a great planning aid.

The person being invited usually asked:

"How many beers, what brand and what's the food going to be?"

Negotiations then proceeded until agreement was reached on all the important items as well as a time and place for the session. As the "planners" showed up, beer and food was passed out and serious planning started, generally with something along the lines of:

"Boy, just imagine diving in 80 degree water, without a wet suit!" and "can you imagine finishing a dive and then lying in the sun slathered with sun tan oil?"

These planning sessions usually lasted about two or three hours, and by the end of each of them another dive had been planned. After half a dozen sessions, someone piped up with:

"Now that we've got the dives all planned, maybe we should give some thought to how we're going to lug all our stuff across the continent to get to the boat." Details.

Someone else added:
"How many cabins on this boat? How long will the trip take. I've got to get time off work. What type of clothes should we take?" More details.

Then:
"Who's going to do the cooking? Where are we going to buy our food and supplies? What's this going to cost us? Are there any small boats on board for diving tenders? When are we going to leave?" Even more details and these details were degenerating into minutia.

No real answers

Of course I had no answers to any of the questions. I like to look at the "broad strokes" of a project, but reality came calling. By the way, the dive planning, which was great fun, never did translate into actual dives. The actual dives were far better. Looking back on the planning experience it was obvious we were so excited about such a great opportunity it took us a few months to settle down and do it right.

Since Bob Blackmore, the owner, had been to Caraquet, New Brunswick, and had inspected the boat, we burned up the phone lines gathering information. He also kept adding tools etc., to the list.

Time off work

Since all of our group either worked or was in school, arranging time off for the trip was one of the first priorities. Various people adopted different approaches. In my case I simply went to my boss, Stewart McMorran, the then Vancouver City Prosecutor, and asked. He agreed and then the real work started. Form after form to be filled in. Government job.

One of our number, John, an engineer with a multinational industrial gas supplier, had heard that, as a matter of policy, his company did not give unpaid time off. He gave the matter some thought and then marched into the branch manager's office and laid his company car keys on the manager's desk. In response to the manag-

Fort Ross *in the Arctic. Note sail boat shape of the hull. Photo: Hudson's Bay Archives, Provincial Archives of Manitoba.*

er's question as to "what was this about," he announced he wanted time off and told him about the trip. The manager simply restated the company policy. John turned and started to leave the office. The manager reminded John he had forgotten his car keys. John paused and said he, in fact, had not forgotten them. The manager got the picture. John was either going to get the time off or quit, and he was the only engineer in that office with a speciality the company needed. Negotiations began and John got his time off.

John used the same technique a number of years later when the company wanted to transfer him to Toronto and he didn't want to go. As with most people on the west coast, when they are told their job requires that they move east, they figure they are being punished. The car keys approached worked then too.

A ton of equipment

Then we had to decide how we would get the crew and about a ton of gear (it actually turned out to be almost two tons) across the continent, a distance of about 4,000 miles (6,440KM). Given the amount of gear the train seemed like a good method. However, at that time, the only train that ran clear across the country was the Canadian National Railway, the "CN" as it was referred to, and it was owned and operated by the Canadian government.

The Canadian government was notorious in those days for using the CN as a political tool to keep the manufacturers in Ontario and Quebec happy by making sure it cost far more, in some cases twice a much, to ship the same product from West to East as it did from East to West. As a concrete example I had a marine stove shipped from the East to Vancouver and

the shipping cost was about $30. The manufacturer shipped me the wrong model, so I put it back into the same shipping crate and shipped it back. The return trip cost more than $60!

The government's justification for this approach was that it cost more to go from West to East because of the extra cost of fuel hauling the freight up and over the mountains. It appears the government felt that, somehow, the mountains simply flattened out for the trains going from East to West.

Armed with the above knowledge we anonymously contacted the CN ticketing department and got the prices for the crew tickets. We then asked about shipping a couple of tons of equipment. The cost of that was more than the cost of the crew tickets.

After discussions with the crew to determine what type of ticket each wanted, coach, roomette, bedroom etc., I called back to CN ticketing, and asked, casually, about "luggage" and was told there was no problem with "personal items" as long as they went into the baggage car. I made a note of the ticket agent's name for possible later use.

Additional 'personal' items

There are those who might argue dive compressors, high speed inflatables, outboard motors, hundreds of pounds of tools, air drying agents, various gauges and high pressure air hoses are not "personal items". It's all in the interpretation.

Anyone who is involved in shipping material around the country can understand the concerns we had about our luggage getting lost on the four day trip from the west coast to the east

Arriving at the train station with our personal gear.

coast. It's one thing to for an airline to lose a bag. It's usually found quickly and, within a day it is reunited with its owner. If the baggage car containing our "personal items" got shunted off onto a siding somewhere along the way, it could take weeks or even months to find it and get it to us. Remember this was in the days before computer tracking.

Armed with all of the above information, two days before pulling out of Vancouver I went down to the rail station directly to the baggage manager. I explained we had a group of 12 people traveling with a "fair bit" of luggage and offered to load it onto the baggage wagons ourselves, "if it would make things easier for him." He thought that was a great idea. He also, in response to another question, told me how much lead time the baggage car loaders would need to off load the baggage from the wagons into the baggage car.

Timing was important

This timing was important, since I knew once he saw the "personal items" he would want to, at the very least, call his superior for instructions and we simply could not afford to pay freight rates.

The plan was to load the baggage wagons at the last possible minute. That way if the baggage handlers, seeing the mound of luggage, became suspicious they would simply proceed and load the car rather than delay the train's departure while they tried to find someone in authority.

Onlookers must have wondered why 12 people, and their "personal items", showed up in a convoy of about 10 cars and a cube van. One of the crew and I had gone to the station earlier and pulled the luggage carts up to the drop off zone. These carts were eight feet long, four feet wide and mounted on four large, spoked, wooden wheels. They looked like a huge wagon, with a six foot handle attached to steerable front wheels, and had four foot racks at the front and rear of the deck.

We loaded three of them and wheeled them

down to the baggage car. Everyone else, with their personal gear required for the trip, hopped onto the train. The baggage loaders look suspiciously at the wagons and I told the fellow who seemed to be the foreman that we were part of a "large group" going across the country and we had loaded the wagons for them with the "okay from the baggage super". I offered our help in loading the "luggage" into to the car. The foreman agreed so I waived the two others with me to give a hand while I talked with the foreman. They muttered something about me doing all the organizing and them doing all the work. Seemed like a fair division of labor to me.

Possible baggage car changes

I quizzed the foreman about any baggage car changes on the trip across the country. He told me that all baggage would be offloaded, in Montreal, from the car now on the train to another baggage car since we were changing trains there. I asked if we would be able to help with that process to make sure our baggage got on the right train.

He laughed and said that the baggage handlers in Montreal were "hard core union" and he thought we would have great difficulty. I asked him if he had any objection to us helping in Montreal. He laughed again and said it didn't matter to him. I noted his name from his coveralls. I also noted the baggage car number.

At each major stop across the country one of us got off the train, wandered along the station platform and checked that the baggage car had not been uncoupled and shunted onto a siding. The system worked very well, except that the train schedule was not geared to normal sleeping patterns. Going out onto a station platform in the dark and fighting a biting cold to check the car was guaranteed to snap one awake instantly.

Other crew members piled off the train to replenish our drinking "supplies" and perhaps buy snack food.

The trip across the continent

A trip from coast to coast on the longest railway in the world almost defies description. The train left Vancouver, in April, where grass was growing, flowers blooming, trees budding and clawed its way up and over the mountain spine of North America. There was no green grass or blooming flowers on the other side. We de-

scended from the mountains and clickity-clacked our way across the prairies. At Winnipeg the temperature was -20F (-28 C) where both exhaled breath and nose hairs froze instantly.

The train then wandered across lake studded northern Ontario and Quebec and pulled into Montreal. The lakes were frozen over of course. At Montreal we changed trains and wound our way along the south shore of the St. Lawrence River to Bathurst, New Brunswick, where it was still cold and ice was still on the lakes and smaller rivers.

The trains we traveled on were equipped with excellent bar cars, a scenic dome car and first class dining cars. The food was generally excellent, served on real china, flanked with sterling silver utensils. Tables were covered with crisp, white linen table cloths and the linen napkins were rolled and held in place with sterling silver napkin rings. Those were the days!

Above: The author in Montreal doing what many of the crew said he did best–pointing out work for others to do! Opposite: Crew member in front of our Canadian National locomotive.

Oh yes, in Montreal the baggage handlers were no real problem. We offered to help and they happily, albeit cautiously, accepted. They had never seen anyone actually wanting to help with baggage. They were also curious about how we got so much "stuff" on as personal baggage. I waved vaguely back to the train and told them we had a "large group" on board.

When we arrived at Bathurst, end of track for us, we offloaded the gear into a five ton truck Bob had procured and it trundled off down the road to Caraquet, about 90 miles away.

Then the shopping for provisions began. My then wife, Ann, had prepared a list of supplies required, but it still seemed to take hours for her to do the shopping. I remember being very frustrated by the process.

One has to remember that this was more than 30 years ago and men, in those "unenlightened"days, paid very little attention to cooking and, therefore, shopping.

Looking back on it I'm surprised she didn't kill me as I stomped around continually asking her if "we were done yet." Again looking back, it reminds me of the current auto commercials where a bunch of spoiled rotten kids are continually whining to their parents:

"Are we there yet?"

With shopping completed we headed off to Caraquet and our first look at *Fort Ross*, our home for the next couple of months.

Fort Ross. *First day on board.*

Section 5

We Meet *Fort Ross*

I'm sure each of the crew had a different impression of *Fort Ross* when we first saw her. She had spent the previous few years acting as a herring packer for one of the local fish processing plants. Most of her last cargo of herring had been pumped to the processing plant and ground into fertilizer and fish flour. A few remained on board

My first impression of the vessel, as I looked at her across the ice packed against the hull, was the elegance of her sheer line. There was just something about her that quietly stated "pedigree", but it was more than three decades before I found out why I had that impression. I was jarred back to reality by the comment of one of the crew. "She's a derelict!"

Fort Ross did, indeed, have a tired, worn look about her. In fact it appeared that even the paint on her deck house was trying to "abandon ship." She had the hull

of a working vessel, one that had worked hard and long. Her black hull paint was scraped, her planking gouged and scarred and a cable staying one of the masts that made up her lifting gear was broken and hung dejectedly from the mast top. The herring scaler, still attached to the front of the wheel house, looked like it was trying to jump overboard. Overall it was fair to say that the vessel had seen better days. However, there was still something about her...

Fort Ross *in the ice again, and this was in the month of May!*

Fort Ross – herring scaler still in place.

any good, or can it be junked?"

There were many clean-up functions that were memorable but two come immediately to mind. The main engine starting motor was a small air turbine. The air to power it came from a compressor mounted on the main engine. That compressor pumped the air through a 2" pipe to a large air receiver, nothing more than a tank really, attached to the engine room sidewall. As one of the crew reached up, grabbed the pipe with both hands, to swing himself over the engine it disintegrated in his hands. He became our resident pipe fitter.

Then there was the "toilet"

The second cleanup function related to the toilet. I know on a boat the facility is usually termed a "head" but in this case I use the term "toilet" because that's exactly what had been installed on the main deck level - a standard household flush toilet. The discharge went down vertically through the deck, made a sweeping 90 degree turn to the horizontal, and discharged over the side - about five feet above the waterline.

When we arrived on board the pump that pumped water to the toilet tank was not working, so the toilet could not be flushed, and, in

As we trooped on board and did our first wander through the vessel it became apparent that we were one cabin short, because one of them was filled, floor to ceiling, with "spares". That meant that two people had to stay in a motel and my then wife and I chose to make the "sacrifice". How we envied those who stayed on board, with very little heat, no showers, and a couple of miles from anywhere. We were forced to put up with central heat, plenty of hot water, and daily maid service. There were also a couple of restaurants near the motel.

There were a dozen people, full of energy after being cooped up in a train for almost five days, so we had to find an organized outlet for that energy. The obvious first step was to clean up, so we divided the ship up into sections and started. Poor Bob Blackmore. He was kept busy running from place to place answering the same questions. "What's this and is it fact had not been flushable for some months. Someone, months before, had used the facility, found it did not flush, and simply pulled up his pants and walked away. With everyone on board, a working head was a necessity.

Just as I was wrestling with the problem of who to "volunteer" to clean up the dried mess, one crewman actually did volunteer. I can still see him kneeling in front of the bowl, knife in hand, slowly scraping the inside of the bowl.

That's an overboard discharge

Once the toilet bowl was cleaned we rigged a rope and bucket, dipped water out of the ocean, between the boat and the dock, where there was no ice, and filled up the toilet tank. We then had an operating head. Of course the discharge above the water line did create some "sight pollution" on the ice that pinned the *Fort Ross* to the dock. However as long as we bucketed salt water into the toilet tank we had a fully operational unit. Within a couple of days the cleanup had reached the point where things were actually approaching "clean". As the cleaning progressed a local stove mechanic came down to the ship and soon the huge diesel stove was pumping out heat, hot food and hot water.

Amazing scantlings

While cleaning and stove repair was going on I decided to examine the hull structure from the inside and, grabbing my trusty ice pick, crawled around the holds, engine room and lazarette. I was amazed at the size of the material used but what astounded me was that, where the interior ceiling had been removed, the ribs of the vessel were closer together than my eight inch hand span. I hauled out my tape

measure and found that the spacing between the ribs was six inches! I had never seen a wooden vessel where the ribs were so closely spaced.

I had also never been on a wooden vessel where the inside of the ribs was continuously planked with material as thick as, and in some cases thicker than, the hull planking. Everywhere I went I drove the ice pick into the wood, looking for dry rot. I must have driven that ice pick into 200 different areas and didn't find any rot below deck.

Herring

There was something else I noted. We had been told the vessel had been used as a herring packer by the previous owners and there was plenty of evidence to back that up. Frozen herring carcasses were everywhere, but, being frozen, they didn't smell. I knew when we got into the tropics the situation would change rapidly, so we gathered up as many carcasses as we could and threw them overboard. The local crabs had a feast. We could not, of course, get them all, so the remainder "ripened" as we got into the tropics and the smell went away slowly as they completely dried.

We also had to consider the question of language. The working language in that part of New Brunswick, is French. When Bob got there, some time ahead of the rest of us, he found his French was more than a little "rusty". It was in fact, seriously corroded. His solution to making himself understood was to shout louder in English. That, of course, is not a good solution. I had lived for five years in the province of Quebec and my French was passable - barely. So, when required, I became a translator.

The kid on the bike

The first thing I did was hire a local kid, about 12, with a bicycle, to run errands. The wharf the *Fort Ross* was tied to was connected to land, and the fish plant, with its machine shop, stores, etc., by a pier about a mile long. The kid on the bicycle made the trip back and forth a lot quicker than we could walk. He also did pickups at the local stores but he worked intermittently, showing up some days and not others. We also made use of a local taxi for the more serious errands.

Work was constant. Local plumbers, pipe-fitters, refrigerator and freezer technicians, all made their way to the ship to do repairs. There were an endless number of small electric motors to rebuild, large hydraulic pumps and motors to fix, seemingly miles of piping and wiring to be replaced, bunks to be built, rotten tanks to be removed, lifting gear to be tested, and electronics to be installed.

There were three months of galley supplies for 12 people to be organized and stowed. Then, of course there was the beer. There wasn't near enough space in the fridge for all the beer required. We finally determined that the coolest place on the ship would be in the lazarette, so that was going to become the beer "cooler." That meant proper shelving. But since we were much longer at the dock than originally antic-ipated, the initial beer supply had dried up, so resupply was necessary. Another never ending job.

The main engine

The main engine was a V-12 Caterpillar and the coolant had been drained from it for the winter freeze up - except somebody forgot to drain the water pump. During the winter the water in the pump froze and burst a seal. That had to be replaced before any attempt could be made to start the engine. It would seem that a call to the local Caterpillar service-man would solve the problem, right? Not in Caraquet.

The way the system worked there, at that time, was that when the boats were laid up for the winter, the owners called the Cat service man and booked an appoint-

Changing out a water tank. It was a tight fit!

ment for spring service and start up. When we called they were "all booked up." We begged. They said they had to service their regular customers first, and that if they had any time after that they would try to fit us in. Not what we wanted to hear, so those of us working on the engine held a "war council."

Lunch with the Cat men

As we had moved about the town we noticed that the Caterpillar service truck stopped at the same restaurant for lunch every day at the same time so we planned to have one of the crew, water pump in arms, (it weighed almost 90 pounds) drop in on the mechanics and have lunch with them.

The crewman who volunteered for the job was a strong, wiry Australian, one of the smallest, toughest men on the boat. He had to be tough to lug 90 pounds up the pier and along the highway.

A couple of hours later we saw him trudging back down the pier, without the water pump so he'd either been successful or he'd been mugged. He had, in fact, succeeded far beyond expectation. Not only had he convinced the mechanics to replace the seal and return the pump to the restaurant the next day, at lunch, but he had also extracted a promise from them to swing by the boat in a couple of days, after we had reinstalled the water pump, to start up the main engine.

"I had them trapped..."

We all wanted to know how he had managed that feat. Apparently the Cat men were at the usual lunch stop so he walked in, found the two sitting at a booth for four, plunked the water pump beside one mechanic and slid into the booth beside the other.

"I had them trapped," he laughed. "I told them I wouldn't let them out until we arrived at an arrangement. I also offered to buy lunch, not only today, but tomorrow, when I pick up the pump."

So the scramble was on to get the engine ready to fire up. As I noted earlier the engine was an air start, but the piping had to be replaced. Then, of course, the air compressor to recharge the air receiver was attached to the engine and until it started that compressor couldn't produce air. So we replaced the piping and rigged the diving compressor to dump its air into the engine starter air receiver. After testing and repairing a few air leaks the system was, literally, air tight.

The fuel lines to the engine had to be bled, primary and secondary fuel filters checked and cleaned and injectors bled. Then the entire engine fuel system had to be primed. We also had to do a more thorough job of cleaning up the engine room, installing better lighting and improving ventilation.

At lunch the next day the water pump, complete with new seal, was picked up and the time set for the mechanics to return for start up. The pump was bolted in and all systems rechecked.

The mechanics show up

Finally, at the appointed time the mechanics showed up. They disappeared down the ladder into the engine room, with a couple of the crew and Bob. The rest of us, save one, gathered on deck looking up at the stack, waiting for the first puff of exhaust smoke. The one not checking for exhaust smoke was stationed at the engine cooling discharge pipe to make sure that, if the engine started, the water pump was working and that would be evident by the cooling water discharging over the side.

After what seemed like half an hour, but was probably only ten minutes, we heard the high pitched whine of the air starter and a few seconds later a low rumble as the big Cat clattered into life. At the same time a large plume of black soot burped out of the stack. The soot was exhaust residue that had settled in the stack since the engine had last run.

Another couple of seconds and the crewman at the engine cooling discharge pipe sang out that water was flowing. A few more seconds and the exhaust turned blue, and then almost completely clear.

A toast

We were all cheering, shaking hands and slapping each other on the back. Then, as I recall, someone produced something to toast the occasion.

The effect of the successful engine startup on the entire crew was interesting. In any project there are critical events that can either rejuvenate the project, filling it with resolve and new purpose, or create dejection and frustration.

The successful starting of the main engine meant the project could press ahead. The crew had been working long hours, with little sleep, at what had at first seemed an impossible job, but the big Cat's successful startup made us all feel that nothing was impossible. It's not that anyone had backed away from the work, or

had become disillusioned with the project, but the engine startup was a great boost.

Once the engine was started the compressor for the air starter was operating so, after a few adjustments, the air start system was recharged. A word on air start systems. They are great as long as the air storage system will hold air when the engine to which the compressor is attached is not running. If there is even the smallest leak in the system the next time an attempt is made to start the engine, there will be no air. There are very few air start systems in the non-commercial boat fleet today. When the *Fort Ross* was originally built she had two compressors, one on the main engine and one on the auxiliary. We had only one, but we had the SCUBA compressor as a backup.

Running up under load

The only real way to test a big marine diesel, and gear, is to put it under load, but being tied up we couldn't really put the engine in gear and run it up to full throttle. So we idled it for a while, in gear, tied to the dock. That worked fine. Before we left we moved the boat around so we could get the bow tight against the pier and run the engine up to its full power. As I recall we kept it at that for 24 hours. Everything worked fine. During the entire trip, except for replacing one fuel feed line and fuel filters, the engine and gear performed perfectly.

There was another item that was a "must repair" job before the ship left the dock and that was the replacement of one of the cables that stayed one of the masts. The masts were part of the cargo lift system and were stayed by a 3/4" cable on each side. One of the cables had parted and a new piece had to be found somewhere. Needless to say wire rope of that

Fort Ross *with main engine running. Note engine water cooling stream.*

size was not available from any of the marine suppliers in Caraquet. So we had to scrounge.

The *Fort Ross* was tied up to a big, modern dock owned by a large fish processing plant. The plant was connected to the dock by new modern pier, almost a mile long. The fish being processed at that time were herring. The fishing vessels tied up to the dock and the content of their holds were pumped to the plant. The fish were processed and then ground into fish meal fertilizer and fish flour. The finished product was bagged in 100 pound bags and shipped overseas primarily to the Orient.

The plant had been operating for a number of years and, as is usual in such operations, there was a large "scrap" yard out behind the plant where various items used in the plant and on the boats were dumped when no longer required. Beside that yard, in a fenced area, was a small yard filled with new and still useful items that could be safely stored outside. The scrap yard was a veritable gold mine for us. It provided various nuts, bolts, wire, fittings, screws, small drums, boxes, pieces of wood, metal and rope. It also provided a complete air compressor that we lugged on board as a spare for the air start system.

The accounting system...

During one of our many trips to the scrap yard we noticed, in the fenced yard next door, a large spool of what looked like 3/4" cable. It appeared new. We tried to buy a piece of it but the fish plant manager said that their accounting system wasn't configured to allow for that. I explained that we simply could not put to sea without the mast stay since in any storm we would run the risk of the mast snapping as we rolled around. The manager was unmoveable. He did, however, repeat that he could not sell us anything out of that yard because of the accounting system. It seemed to me that he had put a great deal of emphasis on the word "sell."

As we got the various systems up and running the time was approaching for us to cast off, but we couldn't leave without the mast stay repair so a couple of us, without reference to Bob, organized an evening trip to the scrap yard. We must have got lost in the dark because we ended up in the yard with the cable drum. Five minutes with a sharp hacksaw and we had liberated enough cable to do the job. I took the cable grease off the end of the piece we liberated and swabbed in onto the end of the cable left on the roll, covering the freshly cut end. The next day, as I was sitting on the boom,

replacing the broken stay section with the new cable, the fish plant manager came by the boat, looked directly at me, and walked away. I thought I saw a hint of a smile on his face. He didn't "sell" us anything so his accounting system wasn't violated!

We had fun too

I don't want anyone to think that we spent all of our time working. We had fun, and learned a lot as well. There were a few culture shocks, the biggest of which was the New Brunswick liquor laws. Women weren't allowed in the pubs, or "beer parlors" as they were then called, so "going for a beer" was a masculine thing. That, of course, led to rather interesting interior design for the beer parlors. The floor was concrete which continued up the walls for about 18" and sloped down towards a grated floor drain in the center of the room. Washroom floors and walls were the same. The walls above the concrete were painted cement blocks.

When I asked the waiter about the design he said it made cleaning easier. "We just hose the place down and the water flows out through the floor drains." Very efficient. There were no windows in the places, except for a couple of very small ones high

The author, pictured through a porthole clamping on the new piece of cable.

The crew of the Fort Ross *working up a thirst.*

up in the washroom wall. Ah yes, the washrooms. Since there were no women allowed, there was no need for washroom doors, so there were none.

As a group of us were enjoying a beer we heard a knock at the pub's loading door, a door that opened right at the end of the bar. The bar tender pulled a jug of beer, walked over to the door, opened it slightly and a clearly feminine hand reached in, took the jug and disappeared. Apparently women who wanted to enjoy a beer gathered at the manager's home, located beside the pub, and did their drinking there. "Local knowledge" is always an important asset in boating.

Then there was the sea food

Everyone on the trip loved seafood, but we really had no time for fishing. However herring packers, all in the 100' range, were constantly returning from the fishing grounds to offload their catch. I wandered over and asked one of the skippers if we could buy a few. He laughed, grabbed a clean 20 gallon plastic pail, swung the connecting hose into the pail and in about a second we had a full pail of herring.

I lugged the pail across the pier, grabbed a fresh cup of coffee, returned to the herring packer and gave it to the skipper. From then on we had a steady supply of sea food, not only herring but also a number of other species hauled up in the herring nets. In return we supplied fresh coffee. Great trade.

Finally the *Fort Ross* was ready for the shakedown leg of her trip from Caraquet, New Brunswick, to Halifax, Nova Scotia.

Section 6
The Shakedown and to the Tropics

The trip from Caraquet to Halifax did what shakedown trips are supposed to do - highlight the strengths and weaknesses of the vessel. Inspections of all parts of the ship were constant, as we looked for leaks, checked shaft and rudder stock bearings, listened carefully to machinery under load, checked the bilge alarm and pump system and generally behaved like new parents, constantly checking on a new baby.

After about four hours with no major problems to report everyone started to relax and enjoy the experience. The motion of the vessel on the open water felt normal and reassuring. The *Fort Ross* was finally doing what she was designed and built to do. Hot coffee and hot food flowed, in what seemed like a never ending stream, from the large diesel cook stove.

After passing through the canal lock at Canso we were in the open North Atlantic and discovered what happens when a ship designed and built as a freighter has no freight on board. It rolls like a barrel in any kind of sea.

When we left Caraquet we had planned to go into Halifax to replenish stores and get some of the ship's items not available in Caraquet. Our galley supplies had been depleted because we had spent more time in Caraquet than originally anticipated. It had also become obvious that we had to add some ballast.

There were also the usual problems with pumps that had not worked for a while, slipping belts, leaks here and there, light bulbs that burnt out before their time, and the myriad of small things that plague a ship after she has been laid up for any length of time.

An interesting harbor entrance

Getting into Halifax harbor was an interesting experience with plenty of fog and no radar. Standing on a wing bridge in a cold fog, straining to hear, was a new experience, one I have since always tried to avoid. We also discovered that wooden ships don't show up well on radar when we radioed Halifax to help get a fix on our position. However we also discovered that an aluminum Space Blanket, (also know as a Survival Blanket), if wrapped around the top of the mast, makes a better target. All one has to do is clamber up the rigging to the mast top. That exercise was interesting to watch.

In any event, we eventually got into the harbor and tied up.

Stocking up. Note diesel drums on the aft deck.

"Experts" on the docks

Halifax in those days was fairly typical of most port cities. The docks were crawling with men and women, mostly men, who made sure they "visited" every boat that came in and tied up. Almost all of them were experts, at least according to them. One of the first down the dock, looked the *Fort Ross* over and announced he had been on her when she was owned by the "Eaton's". I asked him if he meant The Hudson's Bay Company. He assured me it was Eaton's that had owned the boat and it had served on the Great Lakes. He was wrong on both counts.

Another "expert" wandered along and announced the vessel was "full of dry rot." I asked him how he knew that. He pointed to various gouges in the hull, a common feature of all wooden work boats. "She's rotting from the inside out," he pronounced. I walked up to one of the deepest gouges and stuck my knife into it. The wood was so good the knife barely marked the plank. "Looks pretty good to me", I announced. "Listen kid," was the response, "I've been to sea longer than you've been alive. I know rot when I see it." He'd been to sea alright, and was most certainly still there.

Then there was the design expert. When I told him where we were going, he looked the masts and double booms up and down and announced that if we didn't take them down we'd "turn turtle in any type of blow."

Port cities seem to be the same the world over. Crawling with "experts."

On the dock at Tuktoyaktuk.

We gathered up the various spares we needed, fixed the small items that we couldn't get parts for in Caraquet, or simply hadn't had time to deal with, and reprovisioned. We also had time to wander around the city, visit the *Bluenose II*, drop into a few pubs and attempted to have a steam bath.

Adding ballast

To add some ballast we pulled over to one of the oil company docks and loaded aboard 250 empty 45 gallon (Imperial, 55 US) fuel drums, secured 215 of them in the holds and another 35 on the aft deck. Then we filled them with diesel fuel.

There were the usual spills and soon the boat, once again, acquired that special smell of diesel, cooking odors and unwashed bodies.

We finished our work in the harbour, including replenishing the beer and liquor supply from bond, and headed out, once again, on the open ocean.

Being back on the open sea was truly relaxing. We didn't have to worry about rushing to this or that chandlery or supplier to get parts or supplies. We didn't have to be concerned about strangers wandering along the docks asking what we, at the time, considered "dumb" questions. We didn't have to worry about crew members not arriving back at the boat when they were expected or "liberating" any more souvenirs of our stay in Halifax. There were a number of city street signs that had to be replaced after we left.

The first day out we spent a fair bit of time checking the various parts of the ship to make sure the repairs we had made were holding, that things stayed were they had been stowed and generally winding down. We fell into a routine of watch keeping, engine room checks and deck patrols.

Crossing the shipping lanes that led into New York required extra caution since we had no radar. However during our trip across the lanes we were able to pick up a broadcast of a live concert of the New York Philharmonic orchestra on our old, but powerful, AM radio receiver. We had the volume cranked up. Our captain, who had been hired for the trip by the owner at his insurer's insistence was, in the tradition of sea captains of the time, a hard drinker. He staggered out of his cabin and demanded that we "turn off those jazz bands."

I have to admit that being on the boat in the open ocean, in good weather conditions, was a truly relaxing experience. For a person who just couldn't sit around doing nothing, I thought I would be bored to death. But I wasn't. There was just enough to do with regular checks and inspections to keep us as occupied as we wanted to be. It was also interesting to note the time it took for different people to "mellow out."

We had been through almost a month of rather frenetic activity getting the *Fort Ross* ready for sea. The shakedown from Caraquet to Halifax was no less busy, and the work in Halifax was at about the same pace as that in Caraquet.

During the first 24 hours out if someone suggested an engine room check, at least four people would jump up and head off. During the second 24 hours, two would jump to the job. By the third day the question was "who's turn is it?" Interesting progression.

Then Cape Hatteras...

Things proceeded smoothly until just off Cape Hatteras where the wind started to come up and the seas started to build. In those days there was no continuous weather reporting and VHF radio coverage was, compared to now, almost non-existent.

As the wind and seas built it became apparent we were in for a severe blow. Cap, who was still upholding the hard drinking role of the traditional sea captain, occasionally emerged from his cabin and ordered "take her up into the wind". Soon we were in 35 foot seas and the wind was whipping the tops off the waves and the crew was becoming sea sick.

A word about sea sickness. Many boaters have been what they call "sea sick" when they throw up whatever they have eaten recently. That's really only motion sickness, and people often have the same problem on rides at amusement parks or even when riding in a car. After the motion sickness sets in, and the motion that caused the nausea continues, the individual becomes disoriented and continues to throw up, only, by this time there's nothing left in the stomach to upchuck, so dry heaves set in.

After a couple of hours of that the victim is usually exhausted. If the sickness continues all the victim wants to do is "end it all," and most people fall asleep or go into a catatonic state. I'm told by those who have been in that situation they lose all track of time and become "disconnected" from reality.

50 foot waves

As the wind picked up and the seas rose we decided to try to contact someone on the old radio set to get a weather report. After a couple of hours we made contact with Bermuda and were told that we were likely on the edge of a hurricane and sailing right into it. Really not what we wanted to hear. By this time we had dropped the engine from 900 RPM, the engine's top, to 50 RPM, the idle. Also by this time the seas had built to almost 50 feet and the wheel house windows, 25 feet above the water line, were continuously lashed with heavy spray. The distance between wave crests had shortened so we had no choice but to rig to ride it out.

As seasickness crept through the crew those of us who were lucky enough to escape it extended our watch times. Even the sickest crew members crawled into the wheel house to help out as best they could.

We had equipped the vessel with a taffrail log and before the hurricane, when checking it, we jumped up on the diesel drums lashed on the back deck and walked across their tops to read the log. We had a safety line rigged. During the hurricane it was far too dangerous to clamber around on the back deck so we used binoculars and read the log from the deck house aft door.

After four days the wind began to abate and the sea started to lay down. By noon on the fifth day the wind had dropped further and the sea was running at about 25 feet, but, even more important, the wave period had opened up substantially so there was a considerable distance between crests and the wind was no longer tearing the tops off. By this time we had "brought her up into the wind" so often, at Cap's instructions, we were heading towards Africa and to get where we wanted to go we had to come to starboard 90 degrees and run in a beam sea.

50 tons of ballast

We had about 50 tons of diesel in the drums in the hold and after much discussion among those of us in the wheel house we decided

that the *Fort Ross* could run in the beam sea without danger of roll over. The other concern was whether or not the main engine could be brought up to speed fast enough after ticking over at idle for almost five full days.

We decided that even though it had been idling, it was idling under load, so it should be fine. We also calculated that the major rolling about would occur during the first few minutes during and after the turn.

The decision was made, so I waited until we were just over a crest, put the wheel hard over starboard and slowly advanced the throttle. By the time we were half way into the trough the vessel was headed in the right direction and was slowly coming up to speed. I centered the wheel and, as we bottomed out in the trough I put the wheel hard aport, "leaning" the vessel into the oncoming wave. By then we were up to full speed.

As we crested and started down into the next trough I centered the wheel. The turn completed, we ran, not uncomfortably, in the trough. We checked the taffrail log and found we had covered a total of 54 nautical miles in the five days of bad weather!

Within two or three hours the wind died down to almost nothing, the sea really started to lay down and the *Fort Ross* became quite comfortable. By then almost everyone who had been sick started to recover and those of us who had been awake for what seemed like forever, went to sleep.

Section 7

The Caribbean Experience

When I woke up and wandered out onto the deck it was dark and the night air was soft, sweet smelling and warm. The *Fort Ross* was anchored and I could see a single light on the shore, about 100 yards away. We were anchored off Crooked Island.

We spent a few days diving in the area and wandering around the 84 square miles (218 square kilometers) of the island. The diving was superb, and our compressor clattered away almost continuously, filling diving tanks that seemed to run empty far too soon. Diving in the warm, bright tropical waters, without a wet suit, was a treat.

The local inhabitants, about 400 in total, were an interesting lot. They were friendly and helpful and very proud of their island, their history and the fact that they were part of the British Commonwealth. The Island was run by a "Head Man" and his office/home had the traditional picture of the British Monarch on the wall

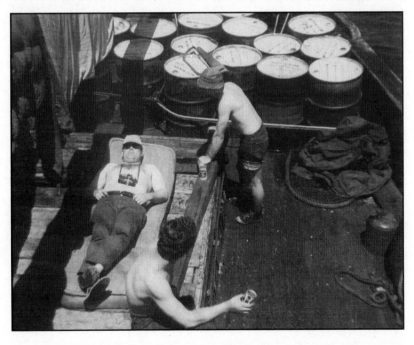

Part of the crew resting in the sun.

- however the picture was of King George V. Since King George V had died, King Edward had ascended the throne, abdicated in favor of his brother King George VI, who had died and been replaced by Queen Elizabeth, the English Queen - then and now. The only postage stamps available on the island bore the likeness of King George V.

It was never made clear how the Head Man was selected, but he had the only generator on the island which made him the most powerful person there. It also appeared that he adju-

59

dicated on all legal matters, determined all questions related to personal and real property disputes, sanctified marriages and recorded births and deaths. Remember, this was in the year 1969.

Blood and bullets

After we left Crooked Island we got a sharp reminder of the fact that Cuba and the United States were having serious political differences and that even then many Cubans were fleeing Castro for any other location.

One day, as we motored along north of Cuba, heading toward the Windward Passage, that body of water between Haiti and Cuba, we saw something floating in the water. From the distance we first sighted it we could not determine exactly what it was. As we approached the object we discovered it was a small aluminum scow type vessel. There were several holes in it but the built in floatation had kept it from sinking. As we pulled it out of the water the few of us experienced with large caliber weapons recognized the holes as those made by 50 caliber bullet likely from a military machine gun. The aluminum around two of the holes was burned black and there were rusty colored stains at various places around the boat.

I had seen the same rusty colored stains on aluminum before, after an industrial accident, and I knew that they were cause by blood. The two bullet holes surrounded by burned aluminum were made by tracer bullets, at that time used only by the military. It was clear that the small scow, and the people in it, had been machined gunned with a military weapon. Who the people in the boat were, and who machined gunned them, was a matter of speculation, but, given the geopolitics of the area the conclusion, for me at least, was obvious.

Diving in the Carribean

Diving in the Carribean was an interesting experience. The water was so clear that we could see almost 200 feet, and, of course, the water was at least 30 degrees warmer than the 50 degrees we were used to diving in. The warm water meant we could dive without wet suits and we did, at least at the start. The salinity was also much higher than on the West Coast and this meant that while we were swimming on the surface we were more

Another crewman just resting.

buoyant than at home. This also meant that our backs sunburned very quickly, and we didn't notice it.. The water splashing over us kept our backs cool. However when we hauled out of the water the bright red backs became very apparent. T-shirts became our diving tops.

Then there was the coral. Once again we reveled in the freedom of diving without wet suits. Moving around in the corral we discovered how sharp it could be and after my first dive I had a number of small cuts on my legs and hands. Thereafter, when doing any reef diving, I wore old jeans and split leather gloves. That solved the problem.

Then the barracuda

When we were planning our dives we put together a "shark plan" that contemplated the occasional encounter with a shark while diving. Whenever anyone was in the water, a safety man, armed with a bang stick loaded with a .357 pistol cartridge, would hover above the divers keeping an eye out for sharks. We used the plan, but never ran into a shark.

However we did run into many barracudas and, of course, we had no barracuda plan. My first encounter with a barracuda occurred during my first dive. I was enjoying my dive in beautiful, warm, blue-green tropical water, when I got the uneasy feeling someone, or something, was watching me. I turned and looked behind me. All I saw were two small, half moon shaped black discs, about 4inches apart. I thought they were simply a product of the brightness of the water and the sun above.

I continued to putter along the small coral reef when I again felt as if I was being observed. I turned and this time I saw several pairs of black discs and they were much closer. I gripped my bang stick and turned my body to face the discs. The discs disappeared as I swam toward them and were replaced by several barracuda, a couple up to four feet long! They were almost the same color as the water, and because of my inexperience I did not notice the fish the first time I turned. The black discs were created by the internal refraction of the light in the barracudas eyes when they faced me head on. I could make out the full shape of the fish if I looked carefully.

Aggressive fish - large teeth

These fish were very aggressive and they seemed to have a mouth half the length of their body filled with sharp teeth the diameter of knitting needles. They also seemed to know when a diver was carrying a spear gun, because they stayed out of range. Two of our group were diving off the beach, in very shallow water, with cameras rather than spear guns and were forced to back out of the water onto the beach. The fish continued to track them until its belly rubbed on the sandy bottom.

On one of the islands I spoke with a local free diver who made a living diving for conch. He had an old, rather nasty injury to one of his forearms. I asked him if it was a result of an encounter with a shark. "No, mahn," he said, "barracuda." "Sharks no problem around here, but the 'cudas very dangerous. Hard to see and slashers." He went on to explain that a barracuda's attack is very fast, and the fish simply tears off a piece of flesh as it slashes past and is gone. He looked at my stainless Tudor diving watch and said "they like shiny objects." From then on we taped over any shiny objects with black tape or simply didn't wear them while diving.

Seafood - fish and lobster

The warm waters of the Carribean produced an abundance of sea food and we ate our fill. Grouper, hogfish and other species which names I can't remember, were easily available. And then there were the lobster. We winkled one out of a hole in a reef that weighed almost 12 pounds. We made steaks out of it. One of the ladies on the trip decided that, since the head was of no culinary interest, she would wrap it in plastic and save it. She didn't tell us of her plan and she stowed it under her bunk.

In a few days the deckhouse began to take on the smell of rotting fish. At first we attributed that to a piece of fish that might have fallen during the preparation of one of our seafood meals. So we ratted around but couldn't find anything. After about a week, with the smell growing stronger each day, someone happened to be passing by the lady's cabin and remarked that the smell was much stronger there. When we noted that fact to her, she blushed, went into the cabin and returned with a plastic bag wrapped package. As it was unwrapped it became apparent we had found the source of the smell.

"You guys were looking for fish," she observed.

The anchor winch was old and rusty —but it worked.

"This isn't a fish, and, besides I didn't think it would smell through the plastic." We asked her why she didn't notice the smell when she went into her cabin. "I guess I got used to it," she said.

Flashers and small tuna

One evening, as the dusty sunset was fading into dusk, we heard splashing in the water. We peered over the side, and with the aid of a flashlight, saw schools of three to five pound fish chasing something close to the surface. We couldn't see what they were chasing. However that many fish, that close to the boat, brought out the serious fisherman in many of us. There was however one problem. We had no fishing rods or reels on board.

We ratted around the boat looking for anything we could cobble together to make some sort of fishing rig. All we managed to find was a single west coast flasher, or herring dodger as some call them, a couple of rusty fish hooks, and an old fabric hand fishing line.

The Ship in the Shadow

We rigged a short leader between the flasher and the hook, which we sharpened, and tied the other end of the flasher to the hand line. One of us then scrambled down the ladder to the inflatable and threw the rig into the water. The instant the flasher splashed down it was hit hard and in about 10 seconds the first small tuna was in the inflatable. We shook it free and threw the rig again.

Same result. Again and again. We tossed the fish up from the inflatable onto the deck of the *Fort Ross* where they were cleaned and stacked like firewood. After about 30 minutes we quit. Too many fish, but they were incredibly tasty. Fresh tuna and eggs for breakfast beats ham and eggs every time. Tuna sandwiches, made with fresh tuna, have a taste unique among sandwiches. Tuna salad is also great.

Cold beer in a hot climate—Perfect!

Chicken Souse and 7' waiters

One night a group of us went for dinner at the local restaurant in Grand Inagua. When I say the "local" restaurant I mean the restaurant where the local population goes for a meal out. When we wandered into the establishment, a wood framed single storey building clad in corrugated metal, we discovered the building was divided into two sections. The restaurant was walled off from a back room that could be entered only through a small doorway, without a door. The kitchen was located in the corner of the restaurant, along the dividing wall at the end opposite from the small doorway leading to the back room.

The wooden tables were arranged so that none of the diners could see into the back room. We selected a table and selected from a menu chalked on a broken piece of blackboard slate.

After a minute or so one of the tallest, thinnest, young men I had even seen came to the table and took our order. I order a local speciality, chicken souse. As the young man left and headed to the kitchen, another tall thin young man emerged from the back room. It turned out the two were 15 year old identical twins.

To put their height into perspective, the building was an open ceiling structure with the traditional 2"x6" beams eight feet from the floor and when one of these guys put their hands over their heads, one on each side of a beam and clasp their hands, the beam ran between their head and their hands. They would have been deadly in pickup basketball.

Since there was no real separation between the customers and the kitchen we could watch our food being prepared. The stove was a very old, but serviceable, propane fired unit and all cooking was done in large cast iron fry pans and pots. We watched as fresh chicken was chopped and dumped into one of the large fry pans, but we didn't see the grease spatter usually associated with fried food. Clearly the chicken was being cooked in something different. Every once on a while we'd see the cook through in some spices.

When the chicken arrived at our table we could see that it was more basted than fried. It was moist and tender and tasted better than any chicken that I had tasted. I asked one of the twins what the cooking base was and he told us it was pure, fresh squeezed lime juice. I've tried for years to duplicate the recipe, without success, so clearly the spices added make the difference.

Jamaica

When we arrived in Jamaica, which had become politically independent a few years before, the country was just in the process of becoming "managerially" independent. By that I mean many of British managers in the various state run enterprises had been replaced by Jamaicans. The operations of the airport and the telephone system were two very good examples. The terminal building at the airport was a mess. It appeared that no janitorial work had been done in months. All the trash barrels were overflowing, the toilets plugged and at least half of the washrooms sink faucets leaked.

None of the payphones we tried worked and at least half of the phones in offices and hotels were dead. Street stop lights worked part time. Garbage pickup in the street seemed to be sporadic.

I was surprised by those conditions, particularly since Jamaica was promoting itself as a destination tourist attraction. I asked a Jamaican manager of a private business why conditions in the public building and public services were so bad. I expected the usual response that the British didn't train Jamaicans as managers so when they pulled out there was no trained management. "Black man's work" he responded. Of course that made no sense to me so I asked for an explanation. I'll never forget his response:

"When the politicians were arguing the benefits of independence they told the people that when the British left, Jamaicans would become managers rather than simply doing menial tasks. As soon as the British left the fellows who did janitorial work in the various public buildings felt they should be 'managers' and refused to sweep the floors, clean the toilets and fix the phones. They term that type of work as 'Black man's work' and simply refused to do it."

When I suggested that, since almost 100 percent of the island's population was black, such an attitude was going to be a problem, he shrugged and said everyone was well aware of that but the government was not able to do anything about it.

Private sector business

In the private sector the traditional management structure was still in place, with the senior man being an incredibly arrogant Brit and the assistant being a Jamaican. I was arranging for a fuel drop with one of the multinational oil companies and was dealing with both the Brit manager and his Jamaican Assistant. I asked where I might get my diving watch fixed. The manager, in typical British fashion, told me that he always sent his "chronometers" to London for repair.

Shortly thereafter he had to leave the office and the assistant and I were alone. He told me that there was a first class watch repair shop just around the corner. When we finished our business I went to the shop he mentioned. The watch was repaired and ready in about six hours. The shop was a certified factory authorized repair shop for all of the worlds top watches, even my Tudor, a poor man's Rolex.

The next day, I wandered into the oil company's office and told the manager I had discovered an excellent repair shop just around the corner and that he really didn't need to send his "chronometers" to London. He gave me a supercilious glare, sniffed, and went back to his office!

The bus stops

As we made our way around Kingston I noticed that there was always a large number of people at the bus stops. I assumed the public transit system was more efficient than the rest of the public service.

It was only after a couple of days that I noticed that, even though the bus stopped at every bus stop, almost no one ever seemed to get on. Then, later in the same day, it registered with me that almost all those waiting at the bus stop were women. I also noticed that every now and again a car would pull up to the bus stop and one of the women would get in. I remember thinking that the driver must have seen a neighbor and offered her a ride home. I mentioned this to the cabbie and he howled with laughter. He then went on to explain that street prostitution was illegal so the women lined up at the bus stop.

Hated for what you have

In moving around in Jamaica I was surprised at the sullenness of the population generally. Almost every government building or installation had troops bivouacked on the property, outside the main centers, and very close to the facilities in the towns and cities. When I mentioned this to local businessmen they said that in Jamaica, at that time, the hate was not based on color or religion. It was based on what you owned. On that basis Jamaicans who owned land, fancy cars, or businesses were as hated just a much as foreigners who had the same. The troops near all the government installations were there in case of "unpleasantness" directed at the government, one of the cabbies told me.

A few of us decided to rent a car and spend a night at one of the fancy hotels along the north coast of the island at Montego Bay. As we traveled along the highway no one we passed smiled. Instead we were faced with sullen glares and we found ourselves hoping we wouldn't have any car problems.

When we got to the resort area we saw that

Successful anchor winch repair. It was a big winch.

Brits were not well liked, they tried to pass themselves off as Canadians. Since Canadians have never been colonizers and have a relatively low profile on the world stage, most people don't really know what Canadians are like and what makes us different from anyone else. Even most Canadian don't know that, so masquerading as a Canadian is relatively easy.

When the manager found we were taking the *Fort Ross* from the east to the west coast, he told us he had done a lot of boating and, in response to a question, he said his boating was salt water, ocean, boating He said he had been a very active boater at the last Canadian hotel he had managed. I asked him where that had been and he said Winnipeg.

there was a continuous high rock wall between the road and the hotel. Depending on the hotel the rock wall, 10 feet high in many places, was topped with coiled razor wire or broken glass bottles set in concrete. The hotels themselves were modern and first class. Across the highway from the hotel strip was what could only be described as a ghetto. Most of the hotel employees lived there. Senior management, mostly Brits, lived inside the hotel compound.

The "Canadian" hotel manager

After we had checked into our hotel we wandered into the bar for a beer and some food. As we waited for our order to be served the hotel manager was making his rounds of the lounge welcoming the new arrivals. When he came to our table and found we were Canadians, he advised us he, too, was a Canadian. His accent and manner indicated he was a Brit, but I knew many Brits who were Canadian citizens. I also knew that in many parts of the world where

1,000 miles from salt water

Winnipeg is on the Canadian prairies, just a few miles north of the border between North Dakota and Minnesota, and it must be about 1,000 miles from the nearest salt water. When he left our table I followed him out of the lounge and told him if he was going to lie, not to lie about an item so easily checked, or at least to check a map before he selected his next "previous" assignment.

The author—again pointing out work for others to do. Note bang sticks and spear guns leaning against the cabin side.

When the bill for our dinner and drinks arrived the waiter told us "anything ordered by our table was covered by the manager, 'our countryman'." I suddenly developed a thirst for brandy, as did another of the crew. In fact the two of us sat there for some time after the others had gone to bed, enjoying brandy and cigars. The cigars were our own. The Jamaican band that had been playing during dinner had done such a good job our table sent them a round of drinks.

The Kingston brothel

While street prostitution in Jamaica may have been illegal, brothels seemed to abound, although they were called "clubs." This aspect of our trip was related to me by some of the crew who had visited a particular club. I, of course, did not accompany the gang on that outing.

Apparently those heading out for the evening, including the only unattached woman on board, piled into a cab and asked the driver to take them to a club for a few drinks. The cabbie took them to a club that had a very large dance floor with tables arranged along the walls. There were many obviously single women in a establishment. Our group was shown to a table where everyone sat down and order a drink. One of the establishment's manager came to the table and took one of the men aside and asked him why a woman had come with them. Our crewman immediately realized that they were in a brothel and told him she had just come along for the evening. The manager asked if she wanted to be "fixed up" with a man. Our crewman laughed and said no, but asked the manager not to say anything. Our lady was young and rather naive.

As the evening wore on women, one at a time, would approach the table and negotiate with the men. The place was rather loud and our lady did not hear any of the conversations. The woman who had approached the table would smoke a cigarette and if negotiations did not progress to a deal by the time she finished the cigarette, she would move on and make way for one of her colleagues to come to the table. Eventually the men ran out of cigarettes so they started borrowing them from our lady and giving them to their prospective "ladies."

Finally the male members of our crew who were going to "stay the night" had completed the negotiations and the rest piled into a cab and came back to the boat.

The next morning, as we were gathering for breakfast, our crew lady who had been with the guys the night before, wondered out aloud where the two crew members who had not returned in the cab had spent the night. One of the guys finally told her the true nature of the establishment they had spent the evening in.

She was genuinely shocked and then blurted out: "And those women were smoking my cigarettes!"

Ice in the Arctic. Photo courtesy of Ken Burton.

Section 8
The Crew's Own Words

From Atlantic to Pacific:
Remembering the *Fort Ross*

This section contains the material written, at my request, by various crew members specifically for this book. I have exercised an author's right to edit, but not for content.

Occasionally the written material submitted had, based on my memory, factual errors and that's to be expected given that almost a third of a century has passed since the event. In such circumstances I checked the facts, as I remembered them, with others and then informed the crew person of my view of the facts I believed to be in error. If the crew person was not convinced, that person's account ran as it was originally written.

In previous sections of this book I have used quotes from the accounts in this section without always attributing them to the individual crew member by name. As you read this section you will easily recognize the origin of the quotes used.

–Roger McAfee

By Ann McAfee

She sat encased in ice. Paint peeling, the once white wheel house proclaimed "*Fort Ross*". After traveling 4,000 miles we were definitely not about to set out on a luxury liner.

For months our living room, in Vancouver, had been control central. Twenty seven barrels of dive gear, medicines, sleeping bags, clothes, pots and pans were assembled in anticipation of the two month trip from Caraquet, New Brunswick on the Atlantic Ocean to Vancouver, on the Pacific.

None of us had crewed a long ocean voyage before. We filled the barrels with everything we thought we might need - signal flags, life jackets, fishing line, molecular sieve, oil can, bang sticks, dust pan, grease gun, air mattress repair kit, rope, hookah, Avon inflatable boat and 18 HP motor, mosquito nets and books.

As chief cook my task was to plan the meals. The train trip across Canada was spent calculating how many pounds of meat, flour and coffee, cans of vegetables and bottles of ketch up twelve people could eat in two months. With the naivety of youth I put together menus which included such delicacies as Chicken Breast Saute, Beef Stroganoff and Cheese Souffle. Anticipating lots of sea food the menu included Shrimp Jambalaya, Seafood Elegant and Chafing Dish Lobster.

The men also made a contribution to the menu planning. They calculated how many cases of beer we would need.

The big shopping day came. I still have the black note book - 21 boxes of cereal, 36 cans of sardines, 200 tea bags, 60 cans of tuna, 180 cans of soup, 750 cans of fruit and vegetables, 700 pounds of meat, 300 pounds of flour, cheeses, dressings, cookies, juices, jams, rolls of toilet paper and cases of Moosehead beer. Several bottles of ENO were also thrown in.

Fort Ross - first sighting

We arrived at Caraquet for our first glimpse of the *Fort Ross*. The rush was on for "state rooms." Thinking ourselves in possession of a prime cabin, we claimed an upper and lower bunk in the forward cabin on the main deck. We then found the boat had one less cabin than had been reported to us, so my then husband, (the author of this book) and I stayed in a local motel until another cabin, which had been used as "junk" storage, was converted back to its original use.

We then moved back on board, into our "prime" cabin. The cabin may have been "prime" in its location, but since the vessel had been out of the water for some time, the wood had shrunk and we had water running across the cabin sole each time a wave washed over the deck. We kept our shoes, and anything else we wanted to keep dry, in our bunks.

Caraquet was a new experience for me. Here, along the longest main street in Canada, was a rural French Canadian fishing village. Small, two storey homes sat on barren frozen ground. The village pub had yet to experience "equal opportunity". Only men were allowed inside. If women wanted to have a beer they did it in the manager's house, next door to the pub.

While the owner, Bob Blackmore, was going to be on board for the whole trip, his insurers required a skipper with a different licence. We, therefore, had "Cap" on board. Cap was an elderly gentleman who was likely dealing with female crew for the first time. One look at Val, Jan and me and he announced "no women in the wheel house." Our place, according to him was in the galley. We could cook his meals, of course, as long as we didn't store, or open, cans upside down, but we weren't allowed to deliver those meals to the wheel house.

His cabin was on the second deck, aft of the wheelhouse. He disappeared into it and we saw very little of him for the next two months.

Our first "difference of opinion"

On route from Caraquet to Halifax we were involved in our first near mutiny with the owner. We had no radar and we sorely missed it as we groped our way into Halifax harbor in a dense fog. The crew had wanted a radar installed at Caraquet, but Bob was adamant that it would be put on in Vancouver.

In response to this, one of the men spray painted a large bull's eye, in dayglo orange, on the ship's hull, coincidentally, exactly outside Bob's cabin.

Once out on the Atlantic we settled into a routine. Val, Jan and I cooked meals on the large diesel stove. Bob, Rog, Graeme, Art, Al, and the two Johns, crewed the ship. As the *Fort Ross* rolled south, we learned to balance ourselves, eat with one hand, and hold anything in danger of falling with the other. Most of us adjusted to the motion. Only John

The gear loaded for the trip to Caraquet.

Smith seemed to have a problem. After eating he would rush to the rail. When he returned he would compliment the cook, announcing cheerily that the meal "tasted just a good the second time."

Sunny days on the blue Atlantic were everything we had imagined a ship board cruise to be. Sitting on the deck, wave watching between meals, were some of the most relaxing moments of my life.

The fine weather was not to last. Caught in a storm off Cape Hatteras, many of us looked in horror at waves towering over the ship. Picture 10 young people, most university students, Bob, the ship owner and an aging captain trying to figure out whether the weather system was moving clockwise or counter clockwise in an attempt to manoeuver out of the storm. The ships we did see either did not hear us, or simply refused to answer our radio transmissions. Gone were the aspirations of gourmet meals. Seafood Elegant became canned beef stew, often cold. We had bread when the sea was calm enough to bake it.

As we moved south and the weather warmed, the *Fort Ross* took on a smell of her own. She had been used as a herring packer for the two years prior to our trip, and as the heat built up the ship board aroma became a mixture of diesel oil, rotting herring, and unwashed bodies. Cap had decreed that "a ship never has enough fresh water" so despite the 2,500 gallons in the water tanks, bathing was limited to deck dips in a bucket or a rain rinse. On fine nights we abandoned our cabins for beds on the deck.

Diving in the Caribbean

One of the lures of the trip was the promise of unlimited diving in the Caribbean. Our first dives were in the crystal clear water off Crooked Island and Great Inagua. For those of us used to diving in wet suits in the North Pacific, the Caribbean was a treat. I remember during my first dive looking with surprise at my depth

Ann performing the first step for a fresh conch dinner. Getting the conch out of the shell.

In Kingston we were met with sullen glares and in the few days we spent in Kingston I never saw a smile. Men walked the streets carrying machetes. Black Panther posters were everywhere. More than once unknown men approached us asking if we were from the *Fort Ross*. When we replied "yes" they replied "George said to look out for you." George's friends told us which streets were safe and where not to go.

gauge to find I was at 100 feet. All the usual indicators of depth I was used to - cold and dark - were missing.

After some days of great diving we put into Jamaica. That island country, in the 1960s was experiencing the traumatic days of recent independence. As with much of the world, colonial rule was being replaced by home rule. We did not know as we viewed the beautiful Blue Mountains surrounding Kingston harbor that much of the white population had fled the Island.

We were met at the dock by a Jamaican who introduced himself as "George". George offered to arrange taxis, show us where to buy food and take us sightseeing. We quickly learned that George was our "protection" service. Taxis arranged by George were half the cost of pick-up cabs.

George arranged a rental car to tour the Island. Outside town we found a beautiful country living in fear. The few resorts on the north coast were surrounded by barb wire and large homes, previously inhabited by white planters, sat vacant. As we weighed anchor we sang "Jamaica Farewell" with a new feeling. We had experienced a glimpse of a changing world, just as it was changing.

After Jamaica we were comforted to walk on the street of Colon, in Panama, where soldiers with guns kept the streets safe.

"Ship's stores" a boon

When we found that champagne, purchased as "ship's stores", was only a couple of dollars a bottle, we provisioned generously with bubbly and lobster for our trip through the Panama Canal. My memory of the trip through the Canal is a bit hazy - no doubt as a result of the wine. Going through the locks we were tied along side a Venezuelan pirate ship. It was a testimony to our shabby appearance that they showed no interest in us.

As we moved through the canal we were not to know that the *Fort Ross* was leaving the Atlantic for the last time. In a further foreshadowing of the future of the *Fort Ross*, the one place we stopped along the Central American coast was a small fishing village in Costa Rica. The villagers were not used to tourists, but they rallied together and produced a great chicken dinner.

As we pulled into Acapulco my trip came to the end. We had misjudged the time our travels would take. After two months I had to go back to work so, feeling like a deserter, I said good-bye and flew home.

My final view

My final view of the *Fort Ross* was a few weeks later, tied up to the dock in Vancouver. Paint peeling, the bulls eye target had brought us home safely. At the time I felt she was just a ship we had taken on a grand adventure. It was 35 years before I learned of her distinguished career before we boarded her in Caraquet and that we were part of her last trip from Atlantic to Pacific Canada.

By Janet Massey

As a 22 year old student who still lived with her parents you would have to call me a naive youth when I signed on for the *Fort Ross* trip. I just assumed that the people in charge knew what they were doing - the old retired captain who would start off his day with vodka and orange juice for breakfast, and the ship owner, who had the night watch, so he had to try to sleep during the day. This was difficult because of the heat, having to cope with the endless problems and fixing things. This all kept him from getting much rest. It started to remind me of the novel The Caine Mutiny.

A derelict in the ice

When we arrived in Caraquet, New Brunswick, the *Fort Ross* looked like a derelict. She was cold and damp and surrounded by ice that ebbed and flowed with the tide. Pipes and tanks were frozen. It took days to dry out the ship. The main engine hadn't been run in a year and a half. Most mechanical systems hadn't been operated in that length of time as well. Would they even work?

When we did get enough things working to depart Caraquet, the ship rolled terribly. When we went in to Halifax, to do more preparation for the trip, Bob Blackmore bought dozens of 45 gallon drums of diesel fuel which were loaded into the holds and onto the decks to provide ballast. This turned out to have it's down side when we got into warm weather further south. The diesel expanded in the heat and oozed out of the openings, smelling up the whole ship. This combined with the heat, the rolling and pitching, and poor ventilation inside, made for some pretty seasick crew.

We had five days of full storm conditions, including a hurricane, as we headed from Halifax down to the Bahamas. I was pretty naive - I don't remember being too scared. I just assumed the grownups in charge knew what they were doing. The waves were huge.

20 to 30 foot seas

I bet they were 20 to 30 feet high. Starting over the crest of each wave the ship's stern would come way out of the water and we'd be sitting there up in the air looking down into a huge chasm. From the stern it seemed to be 70 feet below us to the bottom of the trough. After a big shudder the ship would begin the slide down into the trough. In the trough we were surrounded by walls of water 20 or 30 feet high.

And just think that we would go out on deck without any safety lines. I don't think I had even heard of safety lines. The racket that the ship made, coping with the heavy sea, was incredibly loud, squeaking, cracking, tearing, shuddering noises, as if the ship was going to come apart. We had to wedge ourselves into our bunks with pillows and other gear to keep from being thrown onto the floor, all the while listening to the ship's noises and wondering if the big timber mast would snap and fall down on us.

The days before feminism

This was pre-feminist days for me. Three of us women were "allowed" to go on the trip. One was the wife of another crew member and the other a girlfriend of a crew member. We were the cooks, the wife who had some experience, was the galley organizer and cooked dinners; the girlfriend, a biologist, chose to be the breakfast cook (she didn't really want to cook at all). I got to be the third cook, doing lunches. I knew how to cook, but the supplies I got to use for lunches ran to spam, bologna, miracle whip, and noodles. Tough to make good meals out of that.

For a while I cooked breakfasts. It was a real challenge - mixing an egg mixture for scrambled eggs, pouring it into the cast iron fry pan on the oil stove. The ship's rolling was so violent that the egg mixture could easily slosh out of the fry pan before it set up if you weren't careful. So you had to time it carefully, hang on, and hope. Nobody was very hungry during the really rough spells anyway.

Finally the tropics

We finally made a landfall late at night at Crooked Island, in the Bahamas. We anchored out and waited for dawn. I don't think I got any sleep - it was just too exciting anticipating my first sight of a tropical island. The sunrise did not disappoint - it was positively phenomenal. We stayed several days, going ashore, exploring, swimming to cool off. The rest of the crew were scuba divers, but not me. So I would just snorkel and swim. The water was so clear that snorkeling on the surface beside the ship, I could see the entire length of anchor chain and the anchor lying on the sandy bottom some 100 feet down.

One way to avoid mosquitoes

One night after dark some of us were waiting to be picked up by our tender to go back out to the anchored ship. We were talking with some local men on the dock and the mosquitoes were driving us crazy. These local men seemed oblivious to them - they would just move their arms in the most relaxed way every so often to ward off the bugs. Anyway, we decided that the only thing to do was to go in the water to avoid the mosquitoes. So we went into the water off the dock (I stayed close to the ladder) for some time until we were finally picked up by our boat. The men on the dock thought we were crazy, they feared shark attacks too much to do what we did.

Our next stop was Kingston, Jamaica where we went ashore as much as we could. One evening, the single crew members, myself and several of the guys, went looking for night life. A local guy, "George", had attached himself to us, and seemed to be our guide and protector, although I never really figured out what was going on with him.

Anyway he arranged for us to take a taxi to a night club, which was more like a house with a bar, out in a residential area. We spent the evening drinking beer and visiting with various young women who would drop by our table. One of our crew ended up staying the night when we left to "have a bath and sleep in a real bed".

It wasn't until much later that I found out it was a brothel, and the girls would come to our table, smoke a cigarette, and "bargain" with the guys. If an arrangement wasn't concluded during the time the lady smoked a cigarette, she moved on to be replaced by another and so on until a deal was made. And they were smoking my cigarettes!

I had no idea what had been going on

Talk about being naive. I had no idea what was going on and it was going on right in front of me! Apparently, I found out later, when I came in with the guys, one of the staff came over to one of guys and asked if I was there because I wanted a man. I'm not sure what my crewmate answered, but I was never approached. Half of the crew had to fly home by the time we reached Acapulco, Mexico. That meant there were only six of us left and I became the only cook. That kept me pretty busy.

There were no storms, but we were heading into a fair weather westerly wind for some time. The seas would break over the bow, sending water running along the decks. It was warm and I finally got up my nerve to work my way along to the bow and stand there and let the waves wash over me. That was a thrill.

Rest of the trip uneventful

The rest of the trip was uneventful, except for two course changes - once to avoid a water spout and once to go after a big sea turtle. The guys had visions of turtle soup for dinner. I was relieved it had disappeared by the time we turned the ship around.

By Al Richards

How green is green? In retrospect that is what comes to mind when I reflect on our venture on the *Fort Ross* with two experienced sea goers and a bunch of university students, and recent graduates, who were cocky, willing and inexperienced.

After viewing most of Canada from the window of the train we welcomed the sight of Bathurst, New Brunswick, and the short road trip from there to Caraquet. One of Caraquet's claims to fame is that it has the longest main street in Canada.

Which ship was our beauty?

No, no, NOT that one over there, Please!!!

Al having a bath during a tropical downpour.

The *Fort Ross* had been laid up for a while and the first impression of the ship was one of dirt.

The first question was how were we going to get her ready to sail? The second was what would our various roles be? I expected the owner, Bob Blackmore, and Captain Brewster would professionally guide us around the continent to Vancouver. But I was even more impressed by how one of the crew, a science grad, got the old Loran A going, the amount of organization it took to deal with every last detail of the provision of meals, fuel, machinery, stove and refrigeration repairs, and the fact that organization was provided by the crew. I was appointed the ship's carpenter.

The real ocean

Green took on a new meaning for me when we passed through the Straits of Canso into the real ocean. My recollection is of being dreadfully seasick but trying to do my share, especially after I noticed Art Monk lying in sea sick agony under the chart table in case the skipper needed another Loran fix, or help with the balky radio. *Fort Ross* was designed to be operated by professional seamen, who were used to being at sea with few amenities. We soon became like them, at least as far as the "few amenities" were concerned.

My bunk was just as wide as my shoulders when I was lying flat on my back and the opposite wall was easily touched when I sat up. The smell from the engine room coming through the emergency hatch nicely complimented the view from the port hole. All of these became details of the experiences we would remember for a long time.

These remembrances were added to those of historic Halifax harbor, Captain Brewer training the crew on "the only way things were going to be done in the wheelhouse", surfing huge swells somewhere off Cape Hatteras enroute to the Caribbean, "shooting" the sun, the beauty of the Bahamas, both above and below the water, and a bunch of "innocents" in a strange world while ashore in Jamaica.

Each day brought us something we had not experienced before. One night a passing ship, using a signal lamp, indicated it had a very important message. We woke Cap, and after a moment, he told us the light operator "just wanted to talk" and He, Cap, did not want to talk and he was going back to sleep. The Panama canal was a highlight for me. I was impressed with the efficiency of an American tug boat dealing with the fact that we had temporarily grounded in the mud. It maneuvered traffic around us so we would not impede the progress of other ships. In Cristobal water was more expensive than fuel so a shower felt good as we entered into Gatun Lake.

As home commitments became more pressing, many of our crew members had to head home. Those of us left fell into a routine that, it seemed at the time, could have gone on forever. A storm off the Mexican coast reminded us that the *Fort Ross* was built to be squeezed in the ice and was not particularly comfortable running in heavy weather. Those hot tropical days also reminded us that the tar deck caulking was for use in temperate or cold climate – so we got used to the sticky black stuff on the bottoms of our feet.

We had an old full band AM transmitter on board and, while fiddling one day, Bob Blackmore contacted a Canadian tugboat operating off the west coast of Vancouver Island and was able to pass on a message to his wife at home in Vancouver. He told her we had been a bit delayed by the heavy weather off Mexico and asked her to contact the families of the rest of the crew and pass on the message.

The trip influence

I suppose it's fair to ask the question - did our *Fort Ross* trip influence me? That's always a difficult question. My then girlfriend became my wife and we have been getting along for more than 30 years now and I think having that time as sea made me appreciate her more. The Bachelor of Commerce degree I had seemed to be struggling with, was successfully completed and was used to help me make the business decisions related to my career as a commercial fisherman.

Most important, the sea got into my blood and brought out some of my Newfoundland maritime background. I am still fishing commercially today.

By John Smith

Just west of Lake Louise, Alberta, Canada, on a section of the old highway into British Columbia, a traveler crosses a small stream. If the traveler takes the time to look into the stream he will find a rock, not large as rocks go – maybe two feet by three feet. That small rock is a most significant rock because at that point the stream divides. The water that flows along the west side of the rock will eventually become part of the mighty Columbia River and join the Pacific Ocean. Water that flows along the east side of the rock will commence a long journey traversing the three Canadian prairie provinces, the Great Lakes, the Saint Lawrence River and eventually join the Atlantic Ocean.

As each droplet of water flowing toward that rock is unaware of the consequences of passing to east or west of the rock we are unaware of the consequences of many of the decisions we make. Ten young people met their "rock" in the spring of 1969 and, without a great deal of thought for the consequences, chose to pass the rock on the side leading to adventure.

A ship which had once been part of the working fleet of the Hudson Bay Company serving the ports through the Northwest Passage, the *Fort Ross*, was bought by Blackmore Marine Services of Vancouver, B.C. She was moored at a dock in Caraquet, New Brunswick. In order to retrieve the ship, Bob Blackmore recruited ten young people and a personal friend, Captain Clyve Brewster, to crew the ship from New Brunswick to Vancouver.

I was privileged to be a member of that crew.

Young people have always been blessed with a joyful ignorance, and we were no different, but we were also blessed with the ability to find fun and excitement in the activities aboard the old ship. Things we would find either difficult or tedious today were all part of the great adventure. The author will tell the story of the voyage, I'm sure, but the effect of the adventure can be seen in the succeeding thirty-odd years as the crew members chose their vocations, mates, homes and life styles.

Twenty-five years after that voyage several of the original crew members, their respective spouses and some family members assembled on Texada Island off the British Columbia coast to recount the memories and the effect of the voyage on the succeeding years.

Some who had been trained for shore-based vocations opted, instead, for lives connected with the sea. A lawyer became a management consultant and maritime author. A banker chose to go fishing and bought a large salmon fishing boat. A musician bought a prawn fishery and

lived at the head of an inlet on the B.C. coast for many years.

Somewhere in Eastern Canada

My introduction to the *Fort Ross* was a conversation with Bob Blackmore while returning from a SCUBA diving trip in early 1969. Bob had arranged to purchase a boat from a division of B.C. Packers. The boat was somewhere in eastern Canada and Bob would need some people to help bring it back to Vancouver. Roger McAfee, this book's author, seemed to know the area Bob was talking about and spoke enthusiastically about going to get the boat. That sounded good enough for me.

Several members of the SCUBA club expressed interest in joining the crew. At one point Bob explained that in order to meet insurance requirements an old sea Captain who moored his pleasure boat at the Blackmore marina would accompany us. With all the people involved the number was now 13. Bob advised us that the Captain would not go with a crew of that number - 13 was unlucky, according to the Captain. Fortunately one potential crew member got a summer job that he couldn't turn down and the crew number was set at twelve.

Work began in earnest

The work then began in earnest. Each member was polled to determine any food allergies. Food preferences and dislikes were noted and incorporated into the provisioning plan. I was amazed at the degree of organization. As well as our own clothing and diving equipment, it was necessary to collect and crate food, medicines, tools, a small SCUBA compressor and an inflatable dinghy. The majority of the packing and crating took place at Roger and Ann's home so many evenings were spent making lists of the items to be collected, collecting the items and packing them in cartons strong enough to survive whatever form of transport they might encounter. During these evenings Ann provided dinner for everyone present as well as contributing to the current effort. Roger took care of providing the beer.

Some of the crew may remember the train trip across Canada but to me it was one long party. At every major stop we re-provisioned the alcohol supply with a mad dash to the nearest liquor outlet. We were given an opportunity to "dry out" after switching trains in Montreal as our sleeping car developed a bearing problem and had to be uncoupled from the train. We spent that night in the bar car with the bar closed. Bummer!

After transferring the equipment and supplies from the rail car to a large truck in Bathurst NB we piled into cabs for the ride to Caraquet. Our first sight of the *Fort Ross* was enough to take our breath away. She hadn't seen fresh paint in a very long time and she was frozen in the ice of the Chaleur Bay. While we unloaded the truck and wrestled the crates and cartons onto the ship, one of the crew, Graeme Vance, set to work chipping the ice out of the bilges in order to trace fuel lines and uncover valves so fuel could, with reasonable certainty, get to machinery requiring it.

French was the language

Each crew member was given an area of responsibility and we learned our jobs as we went along. I had no idea that the language in northern New Brunswick was French so I had to dig deep into my memory of High School French to communicate with the local merchants. Over the next couple of weeks the ice

in the Gulf of St. Lawrence disappeared and the *Fort Ross* was made ship shape. Finally we saw a blast of soot spout from the main motor exhaust funnel and we were mobile. After having the compass adjusted by a local adjuster, we were ready to shove off.

The first two days at sea were spent getting out of the St Lawrence River. During this time we learned about steering the ship, determining the distance to the horizon, converting Loran readings to chart positions and preparing the ship for sea. Captain Brewster watched as Al Richards and I installed the boards on the forward hatch and battened the canvas covers over the boards many times. Each time we completed the job he would shake his head to indicate we hadn't done it right so we started again. Finally he nodded his head to indicate his approval and we moved on to other tasks.

While transiting the Canso Canal we had to pass under a span bridge that opened vertically. As we passed, a motorist got out of his car and tossed a current newspaper onto the foredeck. I guess he understood that we had been out of touch for some time. Later in the trip when we were anchored in Los Angeles harbor with the quarantine flag flying while we waited clearance to enter the San Pedro dock area a small powerboat came alongside and the man on deck threw a six-pack of beer onto the deck while he shouted "Welcome to California". Sometimes small acts of kindness just stay in our memories.

A full North Atlantic gale

Who will ever forget our introduction to the Atlantic Ocean? It seemed that we had just cleared the Canso Canal when the full fury of a North Atlantic gale hit us. The ship rolled,

John checking the diesel drums on the back deck of the Fort Ross.

sounder and followed that line into the harbor. Soon we were in Halifax harbor secured to the Irving Oil dock.

Captain Brewster seldom displayed his sense of humor but two instances come to mind.

One day in the Caribbean, Al Richards was attempting to do some laundry. He had taken a large galvanized washtub and filled it with seawater and detergent. In order to force water through the clothes, Al had taken a tomato juice can and removed one end. The other end he nailed to a pole to form a plunger. He was in the process of washing his clothes with the makeshift plunger when Captain Brewster walked across the deck. The captain mumbled "Damn Student Agitators!" as he passed.

pitched and yawed with its one rolling chock. The waves broke over the bow and the water ran down the deck and up over the wheelhouse. Almost every crew member learned about sea sickness that day as the wheelhouse watches were suspended and the helmsman most able to stand up and take the wheel took it for as long as he could stand and hoped for someone to relieve him soon. Meals were impossible to prepare but I remember one crew member, Art Monk, making himself a mustard and ketchup sandwich - and eating it in the wheelhouse.

The storm lasted until we were into Halifax Harbor. We could not see the shore and as we had no radar on board we were essentially blind. Bob called the Halifax Harbormaster who attempted to get a radar fix on the *Fort Ross* but as she was wooden, she was invisible to radar. Bob climbed the foremast and installed a Radar reflector in an attempt to make the ship more visible but even this didn't help. Captain Brewster devised a plan whereby we headed for the Eastern shore of the harbor until we found the twenty fathom line on the depth

While approaching Victoria, B.C. we were in the Juan de Fuca Strait. The strait was extremely foggy and visibility was almost non-existent. The captain went to his cabin behind the wheelhouse and emerged with a glass partially filled with orange juice in one hand, and a bottle of vodka in the other. He measured the density of the fog with his "mariner's eye", dumped a generous quantity of vodka into the glass and declared "That ought to cut her." As he downed the last of the screwdriver the fog cleared completely and the captain returned to his cabin without another word.

By Bob Blackmore

In thinking back on the *Fort Ross* trip there are three questions that leap to mind. Is it really more than 30 years since we did that? How could I have grown this old that fast? How could we (my wife Bev and I) have been so lucky to have found such a tolerant group to join us in the trip? Bev did not take the trip with us, but, during the months I was away, she held our marina business together, with great skill and good humor.

The town of Caraquet was, at least at the time we were there, rather unusual. It was made up of a single street, which was the main highway in the region. This main street was about 10 miles long, and virtually all of the residences and businesses accessed from it. Lower Caraquet was where the docks and fish plant were located and where the *Fort Ross* was docked. Proceeding away from the docks at Lower Caraquet through middle Caraquet one finally reached Upper Caraquet. French was the language of the town.

Motels were in Upper Caraquet and since there was no public transit, taxis were the only way to get around if one did not have a car. Luckily taxi rates were reasonable but the method of taxi operation was unusual. Having come from Vancouver I assumed that when I piled into a cab in upper Caraquet and asked the driver to take me to the boat, we would go directly there. Not so. The Roman Catholic Church in the area was all powerful, so the taxi driver would almost always pick up some nuns at one of the local churches, drop them off where ever they wanted to go, and then deliver me to the boat. Of course I paid the cab fare.

English suddenly disappeared

I raised this issue with several cab drivers, but their knowledge of English suddenly seemed to disappear and my high school French was not up to the task. I did mutter a lot though.

Then there was the question of the beer. There were two main brands of beer brewed in the maritime provinces at the time, one a passable ale, Moosehead, and the other a lager, Schooner. I was not then, and still am not, an experienced drinker, but after trying Schooner, I came to the conclusion that at least we could use it as a trading item through the Carribean. Unfortunately the schooner *Bluenose II* had sailed south ahead of us and used their substantial supply of Schooner beer as a trading item. By the time we got south we couldn't give our stuff away and, in fact, it became almost dangerous to offer it. My opinion of that beer was supported by most of the crew, many of whom were seasoned beer drinkers.

Cap had no faith in "modern" items

The skipper I had hired, Captain Brewster, who we all called "Cap", was born in 1900 and first went to sea in the age of steam, sail and superstition. His saltwater crust was hard to wash off and his antiquated prejudices drove everyone to distraction, including me. I tried several times to talk to him about them, but...

He, however, had little faith in "modern" electronics. I purchased a new loran before we left Vancouver, figuring that, since both Cap and I had operated the old Navy units that were so popular on the commercial fish boats at the time, we could brush up on the new one and be fine. We went to the government run marine school in Caraquet where the instructor took us through the new procedures. Cap didn't have any faith in the unit. I'm sure if we'd had a GPS he would have thrown it over the side.

I would have liked to have had a radar but the cost, at the time, was more than the cost of the whole trip around.

A "quaint" marine community

As already mentioned the Caraquet marine community was rather quaint at the time. I had surveyed the vessel in February and then returned to Vancouver and completed the purchase. There was a brand new ship yard in Caraquet and I contacted them and made arrangements to haul, paint and clean the ship and have it ready to put to sea in late April. When I arrived in April, before the crew, the vessel was still frozen in along side the dock where it had been when I left.

The excuse the yard gave me was that since the government had supplied them with the money to build the yard, they could work only on new construction. I asked them, rather loudly, why they had not told me that when I phoned them from Vancouver and they agreed to do the work. They had no answer. I had to start working on the boat myself, and the only tools I had were a screwdriver and pliers.

To say that the boat was dirty, in fact filthy, was an understatement. All engine coolant had been drained into the engine room bilge and had frozen solid. So all fuel lines were under several inches of ice. All the tools that had been on board had "walked off" during the winter as had many other items that had been screwed down.

The freshwater tanks had not been drained so we had two 1500 gallon ice cubes in the tanks. Looking back on it we were probably lucky the tanks had not been drained or we would have had a skating rink in the hold.

I found that the only fuel on board was in the day tank up behind the wheel house. With my trusty screwdriver and pliers I got the 32 volt DC generator running. That provided lights and battery charging. It also radiated heat into the engine room.

Diesel on ice is not a good mix

When the crew arrived I ordered a 250 gallon fuel drop so we could operate the generator on a 24 hour basis. As soon as we started taking on fuel a skim of diesel formed on top of the ice in the engine room. Because all of the fuel lines, crossovers and valves were under several inches of ice we couldn't shut off any of the lines. We stopped fueling, but by then the engine room was a slippery, smelly mess. Diesel on ice is not a good mixture.

The night before the fuel drop I had contacted the ship's former engineer and tried to hire him to work with us for a few weeks until we were familiar with the engine and ship's systems. However he had 13 kids and was drawing more money on some type of social assistance program than we could pay so he declined. When the fuel started floating up through the ice, I sent a cab to get him. While the cab was gone we began chiseling through the ice, trying to find a fuel line to follow.

When the engineer arrived he stood at the top of the ladder leading down into the dark, stinking engine room. I asked him if he had any idea which valve might have been left open.

"Oh," he replied, "there's no valve open. There's a hole in the main fuel line. I marked it with a piece of tape." I concluded then and there that we were probably lucky he didn't want to come back to work!

It took us most of the day to chip out the ice, find the "tape" and replace the fuel line. Thereafter the generator ran non-stop.

Caraquet to Halifax - a bit rough

The trip from Caraquet to Halifax was a bit rough for two reasons. The first was that we had to run light and the second was because the port rolling chock had been removed some years before. I had made arrangements with one of the oil companies to provide us with a number of drums of diesel fuel so we would have some ballast, but they could not supply them until we reached Halifax, so we had to run light. There were some fairly large lumps, but we ran slow, well inside the freighter track and sounded the whistle regularly. During that run there were times we couldn't see the foredeck for the fog and spray.

The run to Halifax turned up another problem that drove us nuts. Our main bilge pump kept losing its prime and cutting out. We spent hours tearing things apart, trying to solve the problem. Nothing seemed to work. Then, as happens sometime with boats and life, the problem was solved by accident.

As I came off watch one of the crew told me the pump had shut down again. The engine room was not a place to be in a storm like the one we were in. The engine room floor boards were made of plywood and over the years they had soaked up enough diesel fuel to run the ship on the fumes! Everything was oily, hot, and slippery. The rolling of the ship had churned up every speck of old herring guts, scales and oil. Then, of course, there was the smell and blinding noise of the big 12 cylinder diesel engine.

After taking the pump apart again I got it running and was lying on the greasy floorboards holding my hand in the slimy, oily bilge water, at the pump intake. I was monitoring the suction to make sure it continued to pump when suddenly, out of nowhere, something was sucked into the intake and the pump stopped picking up water. As the suction stopped, the object fell into the six foot deep bilge.

Fishing in the bilge

A crewman and I rigged a couple of long wire hooks and went fishing in the bilge. We eventually retrieved a long necked beer bottle. Apparently the rolling had slid the bottle up along one of the ribs until it reach the pump uptake. At that time the pump did not have either a check valve or a screen, so the pump picked up the bottle neck first and that plugged the intake. With that fixed we could move on to what seemed like a million other problems.

As we approached Halifax harbor it was dark and foggy. Judging by the taff rail log and the clock, the *Fort Ross* had run her time and we should have been about five miles off the outer Halifax harbor bell buoy. I had tried, without success, to contact the harbor by radio, hoping they could get a radar fix on us. We had taken several Loran fixes and the plots put us close to our track.

We poked along slowly, feeling our way in the fog and listening for the bell. I tried Halifax radio again and this time I was successful.

We steamed in a slow figure eight while they tracked us on radar and confirmed our position. That done we anchored up for the night.

The next morning was still foggy and we couldn't find the Halifax harbor chart. We had charts to take us from Baffin Island, through the Carribean, Panama, and to Alaska, but no Halifax harbor chart! We found later that we also had no Victoria to Vancouver chart, but those were home waters, so we had no problems there. As we pondered the problem we spotted a small outbound freighter followed closely by the Halifax pilot boat. Knowing that the pilot boat would be taking the pilot off the freighter and returning to the harbor, we weighed anchor and drifted. In about half an hour the pilot boat chugged by and we followed it in. It's not every day one gets free pilotage.

We tied up at the Irving Oil downtown wharf, ordered a fuel drop and went out and bought a Halifax harbor chart. After all we had to find our way out.

Murder not an option

A couple of nights later we decided to treat ourselves to long, hot showers and steam baths so we went to one of the local bathhouses. Was that a mistake! The hot water ran out after two showers, the steam bath had no steam and the "heat box" was a wooden coffin-like device with burnt out light bulbs. To say I was upset was an understatement! As I cast about for something appropriate to say, or do, to express my displeasure, the lawyer in our group reminded me that murder was not a viable option because the paper work would delay our departure!

While we were in harbor working on the various items we had to put in order before heading back to sea, the *Bluenose II* entered the harbor under full sail and sailed into the old Maritime Foundation dock near us. They were returning from the Carribean where they had saturated the trading possibilities with their Schooner beer.

Fuel for ballast

A day or two before sailing we arranged for empty fuel drums to be delivered to the vessel. We stowed them in the holds and on the aft deck and moved to a fueling dock where we filled the drums. This became our ballast for the rest of the trip. Of course during the fueling there was a certain amount of spillage which added to the general aroma of the vessel.

We finally got the ship as ready as we could and pushed off into the North Atlantic heading south. The early part of the trip was pretty uneventful, but there was plenty to do. Off Cape Hatteras we were hit by a hurricane. It was a miserable five days. At some point one of the male crew members suggested we appease the hurricane gods by offering up a Vestal Virgin to calm the waters.

The only unattached female on board piped up, "Well that lets me out." She didn't specify whether it was the "Vestal" or the "Virgin" description that disqualified her.

After getting through the hurricane we spent some great days diving, relaxing and eating fresh seafood. Then we decided to head into Kingston, Jamaica.

We entered Jamaica through the old pirate city of Port Royal and customs clearance processed

Bob getting a start on a fresh fish dinner.

quickly when we gave the customs officer a bottle of Canadian Club. He said, laughingly, "if you think we are pirates, just wait until you reach Kingston."

When we departed Kingston there was a great deal of confusion. I radioed harbor control and was told that we were cleared to sail. I specifically asked, twice, if we had to clear out at Port Royal and both times we were told we did not. We were registered as a yacht so we did not require a pilot.

As the *Fort Ross*, sailed in mid channel, past Port Royal, the port authority boat hailed us. They came along side and were quite indignant that we had not cleared through them. It took a case of B.C. canned salmon to smooth out their wrinkled paper work.

The Panama Canal

The Panama Canal was interesting. One of the Canal tugs offered to let us tie up along side so we wouldn't have to worry about line handling. After the lock was full they hauled us from one end to the other at full speed. As we approached the end of the lock the tug skipper, without radio notice to us, threw the tug into full reverse. Everyone in the wheelhouse realized that our lines would part if we didn't react quickly. We all reached for the controls and threw the *Fort Ross* into full reverse. The lines went bar tight but with our engine going full astern they held. We breathed a sigh of relief. Had the lines snapped we would have hit the lock gate.

Modern pirates

The other vessel in the lock with us was an old World War II PT boat operated by pirates and smugglers. The Canal Zone is international waters so any vessel can use it. The crew of the PT boat looked pretty disreputable so our crew lined the rail, letting them know we were well manned. When I returned to the wheelhouse the Canal pilot was laughing so hard he was doubled over. He had been talking to his counterpart on the pirate boat on a hand held radio. The pirate crew had told him that they thought we were pirates since we were the roughest looking crew they had ever seen. I don't know about the toughest, but I can believe we were the dirtiest. Some years later I saw the pirate boat wrecked on a tropical beach.

Bob up the mast of the Fort Ross.

From our anchorage he took us too close to the far shore and put the vessel's forefoot on the beach. He then announced that the ship was not answering the helm. I told him that was because we were on the beach. His response was to repeat that the vessel was not answering the helm and asked that we check the steering. I sent someone to inspect the steering quadrant in the lazarette. Everything was fine.

The pilot again insisted that we were without a rudder and ordered that we drop the anchor. I again told him we were on the beach. He again ordered the anchor dropped. We dropped it and the anchor shank was barely covered by water.

After further inspection the pilot announced we were on the beach and he was going to order a tug. I told him that because he had put us on the beach I was not going to pay for a tug, and that I would file a protest. He mulled that over for a moment and then called in one of the nearby "bum" boats. With the boat pulling, our engine in full reverse and the current from the locks we slid off the beach.

From then on the pilot relaxed and we all enjoyed the rest of the passage in the Zone.

Grounding happens

The Panama passage was notable for another event, the grounding of the *Fort Ross*. When the pilot came aboard he was confronted by our rough looking ship and crew. I, jokingly, asked him what he had done to deserve being assigned to us. "I take the bad with the good," he muttered and stomped off to the wheelhouse. No sense of humor at all.

Waterspouts and turtles

During the trip up the west coast we had the opportunity to see a number of waterspouts. There are interesting to view from a distance but not things one wants to tangle with. They deposited huge dragonflies aboard the ship. A number of years later, on our way to the Cocos Island off Costa Rica, we skirted another huge waterspout and this time we were inundated by small, thumbnail sized frogs. They were small, but they had voices like cannons.

Off Costa Rica we saw a very large shiny object about half a mile ahead. It looked like the bottom of an overturned lifeboat so we headed towards it. When we got to within 100 yards from the object we discovered it was a Leatherback turtle, the largest kind of turtle in the world. This one was about eight feet long and it raised its head and dived as we got closer. A few years later we heard about the Filipino seaman who fell overboard from a freighter. He made headlines around the world when he was found a few days later clinging to the back of a Leatherback turtle.

There was one item on the vessel that drove us to distraction during the trip. That was the autopilot. It was a very old machine, the "Iron Mike" type, complete with mercury switches that tripped power to the motor that drove the chain which turned the helm if the compass heading changed.

"George"

One of our crew, a big, gentle, mild mannered man, was our electronics expert, and his battles with "George" as we called the autopilot, took on epic proportions. George had a mind of his own and would operate flawlessly for hours keeping the ship's heading within two degrees. Then, on a dead flat sea, he would put the helm hard over. It didn't seem to make any difference to George whether he went hard to port or starboard and we never had time to declutch him before crew members were tossed out of their bunks and food was strewn across the galley floor. There were many suggestions as to what to do about, or with, George.

Finally one night, after our electronic expert had been roused from his bunk for the third time, he walked over to George's "brain box" and physically kicked him into a coma which lasted the rest of the trip. It proved the point that even the biggest, strongest, gentlest of men can be provoked for only so long.

By Bob Macdonald

We were a group of university students, and recent graduates, with a common interest in SCUBA diving. The Aqua Society at Vancouver's University of British Columbia drew us together, and through the leadership of several members we enjoyed an active and memorable program of dive weekends aboard various charter boats. A charter boat skipper we all preferred - for his experience, enthusiasm and skill - was Bob Blackmore. Bob and his father owned a marina in Coal Harbour and several charter boats that operated along coast. Short term charters such as dive weekends do not a livelihood make, but there were opportunities for larger vessels to be used as operations bases in coastal reforestation.

Bob had heard that an old Hudson's Bay Arctic trading vessel - the *Fort Ross* - was for sale in Caraquet, New Brunswick. Bob bought the vessel, and with promises of a Caribbean diving adventure, lured some of our group to act as crew to bring the vessel to Vancouver. The entire affair proved to be a real adventure and many memories still remain. Some of these have had a lifelong influence.

We, with a small mountain of dive gear, took the train to Bathurst, New Brunswick, in late April, 1969. The Canadian landscape at this time of year appeared bleak from the accumulated mantle of winter's grime. Skidoos sat abandoned where the snow ran out. The small towns of rural Quebec and New Brunswick appeared quite depressed - especially so in the shadow of gilt church spires.

I don't remember much of Bathurst - other than the basement of a hardware store where one could still find all the bits and pieces needed to keep the machinery of a bygone era operational.

My more detailed memories start at Caraquet. The *Fort Ross* lay alongside the dock of ABC Packing - a division of B.C. Packers. ABC had used the *Fort Ross* as a fish packer for she had voluminous holds and with the scuppers wired over could be loaded with more than 100 tons of herring. B.C. Packers had fished the West Coast herring to less than economic numbers and were in the process of doing the same to the previously untouched East Coast resource. The Canadian government's Department of Fisheries and Oceans abysmal management capability remains intact today - some 30 years later.

A hulk

The *Fort Ross* was a hulk - nothing seemed to work and everything needed a coat of paint.

With hammers, scrapers, penetrating oil and soap and water we gradually cleaned the vessel and coaxed machinery back into operation. We kept a young fellow, who should have been in school but worked full time for the local cab company, quite busy with frequent trips to town for supplies. We noted that his diet seemed to consist of Coca Cola and hamburgers. He admitted this to be so but thought nothing of it. The gilt spire of the local Catholic church down the road had to be maintained and a person had to be working to be tithed.

One of the more memorable dockside situations occurred when the local priest went aboard one of the West Coast fishing boats and tried to claim 10% of the catch as a contribution to the Church!

While the fellows worked on machinery, the water supply and sanitation system, the women - there were 9 men and 3 women in our crew - cleaned and cooked. We had many memorable meals of local crab, lobster and the readily available herring. The fishing vessels were offloaded with suction pumps and there was an open standpipe in the line to the processing plant. These herring were some of the largest I have ever seen.

With a rudimentary understanding of most of the ship's equipment and indications that it may work if we had fuel to power up the main engine, Bob ordered a tank truck of diesel. One thousand gallons were pumped into the vessel's tanks but we could find not a trace of it. Soundings of each tank showed nothing.

We checked the bilges, put divers over to inspect the hull and patrolled the adjacent docks for signs of leakage - nothing. The only thing

Bob could do was to keep filling and 5000 gallons were ordered. At about the 1500 gallon mark we started to see signs of fuel on the sounding tape.

We filled the air start reservoir with our diving compressor and called in the local Caterpillar mechanic - the main was a Cat - for the big moment. The startup went well. The anchor and windlass on the foredeck was powered by a Detroit diesel in the foc's'le. This entire system looked as if it had spent the last decade on the sea floor. We beat the drive chain with sledge hammers to make it somewhat flexible and called in a Detroit mechanic for the engine's startup. With much swearing, several batteries and enough ether to blow the engine up, the thing finally started. To show the engine who was boss, the mechanic then revved it to the point where I thought it would disintegrate. The ship's water tanks had been left filled and were now frozen solid. (We scavenged a tank and loaded it into the forward hold for our fresh water supply.)

Not the greatest supply center

Caraquet was not the greatest source of supplies and equipment for an ocean voyage and therefoe we left for Halifax. The trip to and through the Straits of Canso was uneventful but once into the Atlantic we ran into the teeth of a storm. Nearly all were seasick, but the experience was very valuable for we realized the inadequacy of the ship's navigation and communications gear. We spent a long frustrating day trying to find the entrance to Halifax harbor. Halifax Traffic could not identify us in the storm clutter and our RDF unit could hear the entrance beacon but we felt the bearing was not reliable - especially to enter the narrows at the harbor entrance.

After several anxious hours we were able to make the shelter of the outer reaches of the harbor and drop anchor. The next morning we went to the Irving fuel dock to complete our preparations. We purchased better nav gear, food and a deck cargo of diesel in 45 gallon drums. We were unsure of the fuel we had loaded in Caraquet and did not know what the availability would be in the future. One morning an LCB truck came to us dockside and unloaded quite an amazing supply of beer and hard liquor. The beer I could understand - along with a few bottles of hard stuff - but there were many cases of gin and rye (Canadian Club). When I enquired as to why all the liquor I was told to wait and see. We had time to sightsee and talk with locals dockside. Memorable was the Harbor Policeman and his repertoire of "Newfie" jokes. After several days we left Halifax for the Caribbean and the beginning of our diving holiday.

...rolled like something possessed

The weather was reasonable and we made good way. The *Fort Ross* was a bit of a pig to handle and rolled like something possessed. Her rounded hull was built for the ice but bilge keels had been added. Subsequently, they had been torn off during a high speed (for her) tow by a passing freighter as a result of a breakdown offshore. She was originally constructed with gumwood hull sheathing but much of this had also been lost - as I recall, during the same tow.

After several days at sea we left the fertile greenish waters of the Labrador current and crossed into the tropical blue waters of the Gulf Stream. The transition was very abrupt and the temperature of the raw water cooling system shot up about 10 F degrees. Within another day or so we were caught in another storm. Due to the spectacular roll characteristics of the *Fort Ross* - short period and high amplitude - we were forced to keep our bow into the seas. As the storm moved out over the Atlantic, our course swung more and more to the east until we reached the point where we could still hear radio transmissions but could not be heard. Everyone was rather tense.

As the storm passed, leaving us in the swell, we were able to gradually add a more southerly component to our course. Finally we changed course to run in the trough and set our course for the Windward Passage. The roll was trying but manageable. With the passing of the storm, the weather was calm, warm and very humid. These were sunbathing - with some interspersed work - days. As the temperature increased, caulking tar in the deck seams started to flow and had to be scraped to prevent it being carried throughout the ship.

Flying fish and red crabs

Flying fish were abundant and fascinating to watch as they made their short glides just ahead of the ship. Some fell on deck and became breakfast. I spent several hours trying to catch Sargassum weed in a bucket on a line. Eventually, I did get some and in the fronds were Sargassum fish - one of Nature's more elaborate adaptations and camouflage jobs.

We crossed the latitude of the Cape Kennedy space launches and just missed being a spectator. Several days later we made the Windward Passage and late one night dropped anchor on the Caribbean side of Crooked Island. Early next morning we were invaded by an army of larval red crabs which crawled up the hull and onto deck. Within an hour, or so, they were gone. From what I saw of Crooked Island, it was small, low and covered with scrub brush. There were a few inhabitants - all descendants of the slave trade.

These included a big, friendly fellow who rowed out to the *Fort Ross* that first morning, lithely came aboard and extended a warm welcome with an invitation to come ashore. He was 70 years old and related to most of the other islanders. His peak of health was inspiring. After a late morning SCUBA dive, Val and I went ashore to walk the shoreline and do some skin diving in the shallower waters.

The adaptations to living on a remote island were interesting. The aggregate in the concrete used to construct simple homes was crushed conch shell. Conch was also an important food source. As there was no refrigeration, conch was kept fresh, and available, by wiring the shells of four or five of these large mollusks together in the shallows. Each conch was free to forage, but because they could never act in concert, they never moved far from where they were put.

While walking toward a distant lighthouse, we came across three of our compatriots resting on the sand. They had chose to free dive further offshore but had caught the attention of a large and aggressive great barracuda.

The next day several dives were made to take photos and to pry a large lobster out of it's den. It was in the cooking pot before we could get out of our gear. In short order (too short) we raised anchor and proceeded towards our destination of the Panama Canal. Bob was increasingly anxious to make up for time lost in ship preparation and in the storm off Bermuda

Grand Inagua - salt lagoons

At some time in the journey our diesel fuel had become contaminated with water. As a result, we made some interesting - but short - stops as we preferred to change out the filters while at anchor rather than at sea. Our next port of call was Grand Inagua Island. The island had two claims to fame - extensive salt lagoons operated by the Morton Salt Company and being home to a large colony of flamingoes. We did not know about the birds when we were there but came across that fact several years later when we read a history of the area.

We dropped anchor and in short order were visited by the local Customs agent - in full uniform. After going through entrance formalities and paying a port fee we were free to go ashore. At that point the agent removed his hat and now, as a representative of the local bar, gave us free drink tickets. The next day a few of us made a dive along the south shore. The dive was interesting but not the fringing reef dives we were waiting for. Our plan was to leave the next morning but when the time came the main engine would not start. We thought air lock but no amount of bleeding helped. In desperation Bob went ashore and coerced a couple of Morton mechanics to come out to the *Fort Ross* and help us. The mechanics came to the same conclusion as we had but did get the engine started. Our next port-of-call was to be Kingston, Jamaica. A diving holiday was beginning to look a little remote.

We entered Kingston harbor and proceeded to a fueling jetty. In very practiced fashion, Cap warped the *Fort Ross* around a dolphin and lined us up with a decrepit wooden dock. While still several feet off the dock, a Jamaican fellow jumped aboard with a large aluminum pot of pot. We declined and George then offered his services as our agent. We accepted. George looked after our transport, dry cleaning, shopping, ashore itinerary and safety - of some concern at that time. On leaving the ship we were greeted by Mama and her "girls" with a large tub of iced beer as an enticement. Again, we all declined their hospitality - I think. The trip into the city center left a strong memory. I had never seen a real slum before - rusted corrugated steel with each dwelling consisting of a roof and a wall and each dependant on the adjacent building for support. Every second unit seemed to be a bar or a brothel.

Blaring juke boxes were everywhere. The open gutters on either side of the crowned road were sewers, barnyards and play areas for numerous children. The smell was breath stopping. Val and I stayed at the Myrtle Bank Hotel, which, in it's heyday, must have been the place to stay in Kingston. At this time, by all evidence, we were the only guests. We spent several days sightseeing and just wandering about the older parts of the city. George had given us explicit instructions as to where not to go and to be off the streets by sundown.

Time ashore was welcome

The time off the *Fort Ross* was welcomed by all but after several days it was time to leave. Dockside the morning of our departure, one of Mama's girls made a final effort to sell her services. It seemed the *Fort Ross* had been in Kingston before - with a much more appreciative crew. We slipped our lines and headed out of the harbor. We almost made good our departure but were stopped by the harbor police in their fast launch. We hove to and several officers came aboard over the rail. They were quite annoyed with something but on entering the galley and seeing several bottles of Canadian Club on the table they quickly mellowed. Now I knew the real value of our cargo of hard liquor.

The trip to Panama was relatively uneventful, except for a tropical rain squall which hit us one afternoon. The rain was so intense that we could not see the foremast from the bridge. The exposed wiring on the wheelhouse deckhead showed a blue corona around switches and contacts. A bolt of lightning hit the sea surface just to starboard. It was very impressive - an intense vertical column of light. Such an abundance of warm fresh water was really appreciated and most of us went out on deck for a bath.

Although we did not experience much wind, there was obviously some involved with the squall as an hour or so after its passing, the galley was suddenly filled with very large dragonflies. these critters were formidable - their wingspan was seven to eight inches. Several days later, early in the morning, we dropped our anchor in the quarantine zone off Colon, Panama.

Customs agents came aboard to clear us and we quickly determined that we had mutual friends as the agents were from Seattle, just south of Vancouver, home for most of us. We were cleared to go through the canal that day but we wanted to make the 12 hour trip in daylight and also to enjoy the benefits of the duty free Canal Zone. The Customs agents pointed out a center cockpit power boat anchored a couple of hundred meters to our starboard and flying a totally black flag - one must fly a flag in the canal zone. We were told the vessel did not have a national registry and was, in fact, a pirate vessel which the U.S. had been trying to pin illegal activities on, but, as yet, had failed.

The Canal trip

Early next morning, after a day in Colon, we raised anchor, took on a pilot and sailed onto a sandbar at the entrance to the first locks. A navy tug pulled us off. The passage was quite an experience - especially with the knowledge the pilot had with regard to the history of the canal construction. Being on a small vessel, sailing into a lock capable of holding a large ocean liner made us feel quite insignificant and trapped. The temperature on deck was stifling until we were raised to the next level. Barely concealed in the jungle along the entrance locks were pole sheds sheltering rows of military vehicles - Canal Zone was still U.S. property in those days.

On leaving the entrance locks we noticed, off to our starboard, a large cargo-style vessel with a rather massive structure midships, moored near the shore. This was a nuclear power plant capable of maintaining canal operations if hostilities broke out and Panama shut off the power. Canal operation was almost all electric. Once we were well into the Gatun lakes, we veered from the range marked course and went into a distant bay to pump fresh water aboard. We were told it was drinkable. There was only one head aboard the *Fort Ross* and there was usually a lineup for the next day or so. The "fresh" water was also pumped to a makeshift shower on deck .

A bath with clear water was welcomed by all as the water in the tanks was still that which had been frozen in Caraquet. In the heat of the tropics this water had become somewhat skunky and quite green. We left the final lock at sun-

Bob keeping an eye out as the Fort Ross *enters the canal.*

down and almost immediately swung into a yacht club anchorage and dropped our hook. The yacht club people had been told we were a yacht and had granted permission for us to anchor. They had expected something streamlined and glistening white - not the beaten (but still proud) cargo vessel that was the *Fort Ross*. We signed in, stayed the night and early next morning went ashore to find fuel and a refrigeration mechanic.

Balboa not a friendly place

Balboa, on the Pacific side of the canal, was not the friendly place that Colon was - they wanted us out of there and quickly. Bob and Cap took the *Fort Ross* to the deep sea anchorage - 5 miles offshore - and left myself and John Smith to continue efforts to find fuel and a mechanic. We were offered nothing - in a very frosty way.

Late in the afternoon, over a beer at the yacht club, John and I were contemplating the trip in our inflatable out to the ship. Another patron - a club member - quietly came over to us and introduced himself as a refrigeration mechanic. He offered to take us to the *Fort Ross* in his offshore sport fishing boat and to look over our refrigeration problems.

It turned that he could do no more than John had done, and so, on his departure, we raised anchor and set out. Several bottles of Canadian Club went to that kindly fellow. We had sufficient fuel aboard but would have preferred some that had no water. However, from the crew point of view, the dirty fuel meant we made and would make some interesting stops. Diving had been quietly dropped from the itinerary - much to our dismay.

On leaving the anchorage we headed straight offshore until we were about 150 miles out. We felt this was sufficiently out of range of the pirate vessel which had come through the canal just behind us and was in the area. The trip up the west coast was not as eventful as that down the east coast. Four of our crew had left by this time and those that remained came to know each a little bit better. In particular, I found Cap a very interesting person.

He had started his sea-going life as a teenager before the mast on a sailing vessel. He had retired from the B.C. Pilotage some years prior to this trip. In the Pilotage he was well known for his superb ship handling abilities. The cases of gin taken on in Halifax were for him - he drank a 26 oz. bottle each day for a majority of the days we were at sea. He drank it 50/50 with orange juice. As I was on his morning watch, I would, at times, open the bottle and mix his drinks. One day, I gave him straight orange juice. After he finished hacking and sputtering, he uttered the most amazing string of expletives which went on for minutes.

This was only exceeded by that uttered at the time I dropped the ship's bow into a trough with the resulting wave arcing over the starboard bow. It unerringly focused on him as he was leaning out of the bridge window for the noon sun shot. The wave washed him back into the bridge and flattened him onto the deck.

Cap was very superstitious

Cap was very superstitious. Cans had to opened from the top that is with the labels up. Cans opened from the bottom had to thrown over the side immediately. Coffee mugs had to be hung so as to point overboard. The opposite direction invited water on board. There was to be no whistling for to do so would "whistle up the wind." Our conduct, at times, was hardly seamanlike - John Smith, hand over handing himself up one of the shrouds, did not impress Cap. As the trip wore on he became a little more used to our challenging his ideas and we became considerably more appreciative of his knowledge and skills. He showed us a variety of seaman's skills including splicing and handling ropes, sharpening knives and using the chronometer and sextant for finding one's position from the sun and stars. I think he was in his early to mid 70's when he made the trip. The first stop on our way up the west coast was Punta Blanco, Costa Rica. We dropped anchor off a small village and a couple of local lads rowed out and invited us to visit. When we went ashore a couple of the villagers inchwormed their way up palm trees and threw us down some fresh coconuts. After meeting the other villagers, we were shown around and then invited to come for supper. We were very taken by their generosity as we suspected that to feed us they did with less. The meal was typical fare - rice, beans and chicken - and very good as I recall. They later staged a dance in our honor. The next morning John and I went scuba diving from shore. We cut the dive short as the water was extremely murky. Instead, we beach combed for shells which were found were abundant and of considerable variety.

I have the impression that we saw more open water marine life in the Pacific than in the Atlantic. However, porpoise and dolphins were common to both oceans. These creatures are truly masters of the seas. They would alter their course to join us and when alongside, take turns in riding our bow wave. This could last for up to 1/2 hour and then they would be gone as quickly as they came. They could maintain their position off our bow with little perceptible effort and even when they left the bow wave, they easily matched the ship's speed with only a minimum of apparent effort. At times they would show real exuberance and leap several body lengths out of the water. In addition, we saw numerous sharks skulling along on the surface, ocean sunfish and even a few turtles. Albatross were constant companions in the Pacific - I cannot remember them in the Atlantic. These birds were to the air what the porpoise were to the water.

A large Sperm whale

Off Baja California we saw a large sperm whale swimming on the surface on a straight and determined collision course. We assumed that once he was within a few hundred feet he would either dive or veer away. He didn't and so we took evasive action – besides he was off our starboard bow and had the right-of-way.

We put into Acapulco to change fuel filters. As June was the off season for tourists, several of us went ashore and stayed at a beachside Hilton for one night. The next day we scouted the local shops for gifts as this was likely our last chance to purchase items at affordable prices.

We also looked into the possibility of a diving charter as there was a limitation on using our inflatable in the harbor. Soon we felt we did not belong there and on the morning of the third day we left - at least tried to. Once again we had to placate the harbor police with a few bottles of Canadian Club for some infraction committed in turning our bow seaward.

Life aboard ship had become very routine - sleeping, eating and standing watch - 4 hours on and 8 hours off. We still had an overabundance of beer which, as well as canned juice, was our main source of cool drink. The beer - "Olands Schooner" - was rather raw stuff at best and the journey did not improve it. Many of the cans developed leaks and one of the past-times became lining up the leaky cans on the rail and zapping them with Bob's air pistol - this being about all we could to express our

dislike for both the brewer and the brew. The ship's equipment also settled into routine operation. The main engine performed flawlessly during the trip - when fed a steady diet of clean fuel. We had become quite adept at navigation. Primarily, we used LORAN C, but it was always augmented with Cap's sextant shots of the sun and stars. A further check was made by monitoring our passage of lighthouse beacons by radio direction finder.

Long Beach

Our next, and last port-of-call before reaching Vancouver, was Long Beach, California. By this time, there was a real emphasis on getting home. Shortly after our encounter with the whale we put into Long Beach and in the shelter of a great arc shaped breakwater tied up at a fisherman's wharf. A couple of restaurant meals, some phone calls home and a day, or so, shopping for marine hardware – at cheap U.S. prices – and we left for the last leg. Canadian Club was not needed.

This leg was uneventful, save for an early summer storm which met us bow on. The *Fort Ross* was much more comfortable in pitch than roll - at least for me as my bunk lay athwartships. When off the Columbia River, a topic for conversation during one watch was storms at sea and in which ocean were they worst. Cap, who had sailed the world oceans, said the most treacherous seas he had ever experienced were off the Columbia River in winter.

As we passed Cape Flattery and approached Canadian waters we began wondering what to do with the excess hard liquor on board. Each person had several bottles beyond the allowable import allowance. The preferred plan seemed to be sailing through the Gulf

Islands, putting the liquor in weighted sacks, and dropping the sacks on a reef. We would return several weeks later, dive on the reef and recover them. However, we stuck to the lanes, deciding to take our chances with Customs. We tied up at a Coal Harbor fuel dock and phoned Canada Customs for clearance. An agent appeared shortly after midnight and, as we had mutual friends and were all equally as tired, cleared us with a "Welcome Home". The next morning we took the *Fort Ross* to her new berth at Blackmore's Marina.

By Val Macdonald

The trip taken on the *Fort Ross* was a life-changing experience for me. We started out as ten almost-raw recruits with little sea-going experience, under the supervision of Captain Brewster and the boat's owner, Bob Blackmore. But by the time we reached the Panama Canal in this beaten-up historic boat we had all become more comfortable with life on the sea. We had all matured, learned to work together, and have faith in each other. Our adventures on the *Fort Ross* taught us about our potential and our strengths.

But it is difficult to define, thirty plus years later, how the trip affected us: what we lost, what we gained, and what we learned about others and ourselves. It is possible that I read more into the trip than the others may have, for I did have the experience of my life. I gained not only treasured memories but a new confidence in myself.

The most significant experience I had on the *Fort Ross* was during the initial trip from Caraquet, through Canso Strait to Halifax. In the span of one day, I learned to have faith in that old ship, and discovered strength in my ability to face fear.

My fear of rough weather started with an experience I had on the beloved boat of my childhood, *Cleodoxa*. From age six to adulthood I spent weekends cruising the Strait of Georgia, British Columbia and I loved that boat with all my heart . One calm day, Cleo struck a submerged log. It bounced off the hull, hit the shallow channel bottom and rebounded, smashing some planking on the starboard side and Cleo swamped.

To this day I remember the vision of the water coming up, not the boat going down. She was recovered and repaired (and continues to cruise the B.C. coastal inlets) but I will never forget the fear I felt as Cleo took on water. I became anxious whenever we encountered rough weather because I did not want that grand old lady to be damaged.

This anxiety was transferred to the *Fort Ross*.

In the early morning the day we passed out of Canso Strait and into the North Atlantic we found ourselves in a fog-laced wildness. It was going to be a long day. In hindsight, we could have been better prepared.

Loran but no radar

The *Fort Ross* was equipped with Loran but no radar. On the Nova Scotia coast at that time we could pick up one Loran signal and no others. We knew the boat was positioned someplace on the long curve sweeping perpendicular to the coast, but there were no other signals running parallel to the coast that would help us determine where on this curve we were. We had a compass setting that indicated that we were heading towards Sable Island, but the fog was so thick that we could see no more than 100 feet ahead of the bow.

Bob Blackmore made contact with Halifax radio and they started the task of figuring out which blob we were on their radar. Unfortunately, the VHF on board could only transmit. Art Monk fiddled with the ship's short wave radio so we could receive their channel. The Transport Canada radio officer, with the help of this patchwork system, guided us into the outer harbour.

I had shipped aboard as "breakfast cook". It seemed a reasonable choice for someone with few cooking skills, but it soon became obvious that most people preferred to fend for themselves in the mornings. On this stormy morning, I managed to make half a dozen breakfasts before it was too rough to safely handle a hot pan at which point I gave up and supplied the cold cereal to the few remaining unfed crew. I was content with the interruption in my duties, as I was becoming increasingly aware of the rapid movements of the *Fort Ross*.

Initially she was riding fine

Initially, positioned as I was near the stern, I felt she was managing fine. I sensed that her ride was relatively comfortable and I need not be anxious. However, as the day wore on, it became apparent that another oversight was the lack of ballast. The *Fort Ross* was built as a freighter, and without weight in the holds, she was very light on her keel.

As the ship traveled further offshore, the movement became more severe. A couple of crew were seasick and bunkset. I sat in the galley as the vessel tossed and rolled more and more earnestly as the minutes ticked by. Two hours later I moved to the galley step and looked out over the aft deck. I kept telling myself she was doing just fine. To prove this to myself, I moved out onto the stern deck on the port side to get a better view of the seas. I could not see far because of the thick fog, but I listened to the waves, the steady throb of the engine, the chuffing of the exhaust and the occasional baritone of the ships foghorn.

A bell buoy ringing

A bell buoy ringing startled me when it sounded to starboard. I could not guess the distance, but I knew it was close. Then I heard another fog horn sound nearby and I moved to the starboard gunwhale. I had a moment of confusion because I was not sure if I could hear breakers. Then I heard the "swoosh-swoosh" sound that was distinctive of the passing of a large freighter. I held my breath; she was close. My stomach clenched in fear, and I immediately realized the danger the *Fort Ross* was in and fervently hoped that the freighter could see us on radar. My heart was racing!

Slowly the sound faded away and I was again listening to the waves roll and the sound of the *Fort Ross* engine. I realized I needed to pass this information to the crew on the bridge. What on earth were we doing out here, so unprepared! I climbed the companionway to the bridge, where most everyone had congregated. I asked those present if they were aware that a freighter passed nearby and none had heard it or seen it. This caused some consternation.

30 footers out there

I went to the wheelhouse window and looked out. I was shocked! From this height the waves were the largest I had ever seen, at least 30 feet high. This was nothing compared to what seasoned sailors and fisher folk are familiar with, but for a young kid from the west coast, it was stunning! I sat down and tried to collect my senses. I sat for about 15 minutes, watching through the pilot house door as the waves rolled into the distance. Finally, I gathered my shocked senses and steeled myself and took another look at the waves crashing over the bow. I watched the boat pass over three waves before I had to sit down again. My whole world had shrunk into this boat and an eternity passed as I watched the waves out the window. I slowly absorbed the reality that the *Fort Ross* was not going to sink. She was steadily making her way forward, up and over those terrifyingly large waves. Each wave seemed to make her roll too far to one side, but the next wave made her move almost too far in the opposite direction. Although she was a heavy boat she was currently so buoyant that her movements were spritely. There was talk on the bridge about the need for ballast.

Finally, the harbor

Slowly we continued to make headway and we finally heard that the radio operators had found us on their screen and were going to talk us into safe anchorage. Our relief was great. Interestingly, my fear for the safety of the ship had passed. I had assessed that she was a sturdy lady well able to handle the tossing. I was the one who needed to be more sturdy. When we finally dropped anchor in the outer harbour the main engine was shut down and the silence encompassed me. I felt at peace.

We spent a week in Halifax during which we acquired a better radio and ballast. Oil drums were loaded into the hold and onto the stern deck. Once filled with fuel they would be our ballast. Diesel fuel became an intimate companion., as it soon covered the decks, our clothes, our shoes, our gear and our bodies. When I returned home to Vancouver I threw away most of my soiled shipboard belongings.

Halifax was enjoyable

We enjoyed our visit in Halifax, the first few days of our trip without a persistent coating of diesel fuel. I was returning from a visit with a friend who had provided Robert (my then boyfriend and now husband) and I with a memorable trip to Peggy's Cove when I was stopped by an elderly gentleman. He had seen the television newsclip about the *Fort Ross* and he stopped me because he was agitated that we would be thinking of going to sea in that terrible boat!

He spoke of her only in negatives. I would not accept his opinion. I had faith in the *Fort Ross*. She was east coast built and as strong as they could make her. She was for the Arctic and she handled the North Atlantic just fine. She saved my life and I told him as much. He left feeling abused, I'm sure, that I would not accept his opinion. I thought his opinion was an insult to all east coast mariners. They know how to build and sail those great Atlantic boats.

We finally get the cabin flies

Two days out of Halifax the water turned from dark, cold green to the deepest tropical royal blue. We also began to feel the heat and lethargy set in. Even our travelling companions, the cabin flies, slowed down to a crawl. It took little effort to wipe them out while they were in this state, and we enjoyed a fly-less cabin for a few days. When we made landfall at Crooked Island in the Bahamas we picked up more flies. They were smaller and much faster than their northern cousins It took only a few attempts to eradicate them before we realized we were hopelessly outclassed. We were much too slow. On the journey up the Pacific coast, Robert told me how the tropical flies slowed down the farther north they traveled and eventually they disappeared.

Red crabs on deck

The evening that we arrived at Crooked Island was magical. The big engine was shut down for a well-earned rest and the generator ticked over somewhere below. It was much too hot to sleep in the cabin, so Robert and I set up mosquito netting and slept outdoors on the stern hatch cover. Suddenly we were invaded. Over the side of the boat came hundreds of young, bright red crabs. These little fellows scrambled over the gunwhales, along the deck, everywhere. They were about an inch to an inch and a half long, including legs but I don't know what type of crab they were. It may be that the *Fort Ross* had passed through some weed or flotsam and picked up these little travelers. By morning, most of them had gone. I always wondered where - back overboard? Did they think we were and island, and left when they discovered we had no palm trees?

Then flying fish

Our next visitors were flying fish. They were beautiful creatures - they had a lovely rich blue back with silver undersides. Their color reminded me of the tropical blue ocean.

The shape of their bodies was also striking. In cross-section they were triangular at the head, changing to square through the body and tapering near the tail. Unfortunately, they met the same fate as the northern flies when they met with our boat. I cannot express how sad I felt for them dying on the deck. I did not like to see them gasping and flailing. The crew was more practical and cooked the fish for breakfast. Everyone declared them delightful, but I remember only feeling sad.

Great Inagua

Great Inagua was another interesting landfall. It was famous for its flamingo lakes and the Morton Salt Company. Robert and I decided not to make the trip ashore to the pub with the crew. We wanted some space and peace. We wished everyone away and enjoyed the quiet on the afterdeck. Later on we heard Captain Brewster call, where was everyone? We went up the bridge and spent an enjoyable evening getting to know him better. He was a retired, certified, coastal ship pilot and came along on the trip as an insurance requirement. Captain Brewster was the one who insisted that we buy several cases of Canadian Club whisky for the ship. It most definitely was not for the crew. His ship-handling was awesome. The *Fort Ross* had a large single screw and with her tubby mien she was no sweetheart to manoeuver but he made it look easy.

Kingston, Jamaica

Upon arrival in Kingston, Jamaica, it became apparent that Captain Brewster knew the customs and rules. By the time the customs officers had come aboard and entered the galley, Captain Brewster was already sitting at the table with several bottles of Canadian Club

Val and laundry. Note conch shells on counter.

town was expressed and he instructed us as to where and when we could safely walk through town. Robert and I chose to relax and clean up in a local hotel and George recommended the Myrtlebank. We had an interesting stay there. It was a dignified hotel and reminded me of an old lady of style. It felt oddly quiet and empty and we were likely the only inhabitants. We registered and were taken to our room by the bellboy, a handsome, elderly man. We later saw him in the dining lounge, as he was the barkeeper and waiter as well. He was also a friend of George's, who dropped in to see if we were mindful of his instructions not to wander after dark to the east of the hotel. It turned out that the borders of a nearby shanty town had crept to the edge of the Myrtlebank property. It was difficult to imagine that we were so close to a ghetto in the midst of such stateliness. It didn't matter, we were content to relax and enjoy the outdoor pool.

at one end. We were surprised that Captain Brewster had moved so fast, for he had such an easy-going manner. The customer officers duly checked us out, examining passports and visas. Never have I seen official business move so efficiently. The CC was slipped into briefcases as they left. About half an hour later, a speedboat came by and a fellow yelled to us, "Do you have any of that Canadian stuff!?" We played dumb and threw over several cans of beer, Olands Schooner Ale. They threw it overboard. Eventually we did as well for all the cans corroded.

As we tied up to a designated wharf in Kingston we were "adopted" by a wily soul who introduced himself as "George". I think George's job was to keep us out of harms way and make sure we spent our money for the benefit of his extended family and friends. Sleeping bags went with George to a local drycleaners, and he ensured a particular taxi company provided us with transport. His concern for our safety in

An "uptown" night

During our second night in Kingston we went "uptown" for supper at a ritzy hotel. There was an exquisite smorgasbord set out next to a pool and a band played alongside. It was a revelation to taste and drink fresh pineapple juice. It must have been picked and squeezed moments before we drank it. It was a taste sensation that I still remember vividly but have never experienced again. The Hawaiian pineapple we have on our tables is not the same.

When it came time to switch our time off with the rest of the crew, we returned to the *Fort Ross*, now anchored offshore. Bob Blackmore had acquired some fresh coconuts, still wrapped in their thick hides. I have a photograph of Bob in his diesel coated shorts and chest, complete with a diesel stained headband, handling the coconut like a pro, machete in hand. Looking at the photos, we all looked like pirates, but Bob Blackmore looked fearsome.

Jamaica farewell

It turned out as we were leaving Kingston harbor that we had to inform the authorities of our intention to leave. An oversight. We were enjoying the cruise along the harbor when a harbor police boat hailed us as it came alongside. It was customs and immigration and they were upset with us. We all wondered what the fuss was about. Captain Brewster had it under control. He had the Canadian Club ready on the galley table even before they boarded. We explained our oversight and apologized. We were forgiven, and were warned not to leave again with out notifying the authorities. I wondered, at the time, if it was a ploy to get more Canadian Club.

A couple of days out of Kingston the weather changed and we were in another storm. The *Fort Ross* was back to tossing her spray and shaking her works. Squalls roared off the land and enveloped us with the scents of tropical flowers. The clouds closed over and the darkness came quickly, as it does in the tropics. Lightening flashed and the downpour began.

Then the dragon flies

There was a sense of unreality that accompanied the tropical storm and it was heightened when monstrous dragonflies started to fly into the galley. Their bodies were about six inches long and they had a 14" wingspan. They were shiny green and had a prehistoric majesty about them. They were blown offshore by the storm and, attracted by the stern deck light, came in through the open galley doorway. We swatted at a couple of them, and left the rest. By morning there was no sign of them. I heard later that when some refrigerator repairs were made in Vancouver, a dragonfly carcass was found behind the old equipment. Its size quite surprised everyone.

The Panama Canal

Panama Canal beckoned. Decision time loomed, too, for me. I had told my boss at the Institute of Oceanography at the University of British Columbia that the trip would take 6 weeks. I had been away for 7 weeks and was going to push 8. It made no sense to be so close to the Panama Canal and not go through it. I just had to make the passage so I decided to stay. The *Fort Ross* had to be made ready for the canal passage as well. Several long, strong 1.5" sisal lines were purchased and loops had to be spliced and the free ends crowned.

We had to wait several days before Canal authorities instructed us to proceed so Robert and I went ashore and took in the sights of Colon. We had lunch at the local yacht club. It was an odd sensation as we saw armed soldiers at all street corners. The stores had sheet metal fold-up doors. There was a sense of tension, but it may have been because we were outsiders. I found a store that sold very lovely native

pottery and purchased a couple of plates. I had to ask the shop-keeper to tell us where the "banco" was because she preferred cash. It was upon my return to Canada I gave one plate away as a gift, that many years later, returned to me. They both grace a plate rail in our home to this day.

Travel through the Canal was worth the wait. The night before we were scheduled to traverse the canal, we had a long evening on deck making sure all the line-handling gear was ready. These long lines were required for tying alongside any other boat sharing a lock.

Fort Ross moving into the Canal.

This evening was memorable because we saw yet another side of Captain Brewster. He told us all manner of tales as he instructed and inspected the lines. In a way, I regret being shy about talking to Cap during the trip. I realize now that he may have been lonely, and his aloofness may have been his shyness around these college kids.

Modern pirates

When we were in the second lock on the Atlantic side, we were directed to tie alongside a rogue vessel. She was a steel hull boat with a large afterdeck, somewhat in the style of a west coast tugboat. She was painted dark grey, black and navy blue.

At first glance, she appeared military. But the crew were definitely not military. They looked to be a menacing bunch with their skeptical brooding expressions. She flew a skull and crossbones. Was this a modern pirate boat?

I wondered how we appeared to them and looked objectively at the *Fort Ross*. She was a rough looking boat and our crew, with all the diesel stains on our skin and clothes, didn't look much better. The presence of women on board made us even more anomalous.

Back to work

It was with great sadness that I left the *Fort Ross* to return to my job. When I walked into the oceanography hut I was greeted with the comment "Oh, you back so soon?" I could have cursed. If it seemed like I got back early, maybe I could have stayed? It would have been marvelous to see the trip to its end.

Then there was the *Fort Ross*. When we first ran into a heavy sea with her, I had been anxious. As we got to know her, and realized just how sturdy she was, the anxiety disappeared. I like to think she knew we respected her working heritage and that we did our best to clean her up. Bob Blackmore worked hard to bring her back to what she had been - a proud, hardworking vessel. During the trip we slowly gained insight into her quirks. I learned to love that old boat. Not only did she have character, she had soul.

Section 9

Conclusion

Once the *Fort Ross* had a chance to "rest up" from her trip she immediately returned to her role as the hard working vessel envisioned by her designer and original owner. Based out of Vancouver until July 1973, she was chartered to the government and various forestry companies for tree planting up and down the B.C. coast. She also did diving, geological and school charters.

In 1973 she underwent a major refit and installation of refrigeration tanks for her next role - shark fishing off Central America.

Bob Blackmore had obtained contracts to supply fresh shark meat for business concerns in Central America and the *Fort Ross* was based out of Costa Rica from 1973 through the early part of 1975. She fished along the coast from Panama to Mexico. Towards the end of 1975 her base of operations moved to Corinto, Nicaragua.

She operated there until the rebellion in that country. The rebels apparently decided that Bob and his wife Bev posed some kind of threat and sent a firing squad to "interview" them. Bob and Bev escaped just two hours before the squad arrived. However, they had to leave the *Fort Ross*. Unattended, and probably looted, she eventually sank - an ignominious end for such a pedigreed, hard working vessel.

What does one learn?

Looking back on the adventure our group experienced bringing the *Fort Ross* from the east coast to Vancouver, the question that always surfaces is "what did I learn from the trip?".

The various crew members who shared the trip have written about their remembrances and mine are recorded throughout this book. Most of mine are of specific incidents. However what one learns is different from what one experiences, although the experiences are one of the major factors in the learning process.

We all learned about different places, different people, different food and different customs. We also learned that different cultures see things from a different point of view. We also, of course, learned a lot about boats, boating and weather.

However, for me, the thing that I learned,

Fort Ross *and the historic HBC supply paddlewheeler* SS MacKenzie River *at Tuktuk in 1947. Photo: Hudson's Bay Archives, Provincial Archives of Manitoba.*

and that stuck with me, was that a group of individuals, with different backgrounds and experiences could do amazing things when all worked towards a common goal. Despite the different background and experiences among the crew we got the *Fort Ross* ready for sea and brought her successfully around to Vancouver without killing or injuring anyone.

All members of the crew on that trip were strongly individualistic, a trait that seems common among people who spend time at sea. Therefore, in order to get the job done, the art of compromise had to be learned and practiced. Some learned quicker than others. I was one of the slow learners on that issue, but I did learn

and it has stood me in good stead since that time.

The other thing learned was to allow for individual differences and to a certain extent that is the start of learning to be understanding of another person's weaknesses and strengths. This tolerance, once learned, grows into a much broader based tolerance.

The value of good design

It was during the trip on the *Fort Ross* that I learned the value of a properly designed vessel, one designed for the job it was to do. That may sound obvious, but in this day and age of "off the shelf" designs there is always a temptation

Fort Ross and and native boats at Tuktuk, circa 1945. Photo: Hudson's Bay Archives, Provincial Archives of Manitoba.

Fort Ross the first vessel to circumnavigate North America?

As noted at the beginning of this book there is evidence to suggest that the *Fort Ross* was the first vessel to circumnavigate the North American continent and that evidence is found in a small booklet written by RCMP Sergeant Henry Larsen, who described himself as the "Commander" of the venerable RCMP schooner *St. Roch*.

to save money and "make do" with a design that was meant for another application. That does not mean that an off the shelf design should not be considered, but rather that the design selected should be one that fits with the boater's intended use.

Then there is the other side to the same coin. When a vessel is designed to be used in a certain way, to use it in another can lead to unpleasant results. The *Fort Ross* was designed as a small freighter and without the freight weight she did not perform as well as she could. The first part of the trip, from Caraquet to Halifax, was run with nothing in the hold. She was "tender" to say the least. The addition of 50 tons of diesel in drums at Halifax settled her down nicely and enabled us to ride out the hurricane without serious incident.

The RCMP vessel went west to east through the Northwest Passage during 1940-1942, a two year passage. It operated as a floating police detachment during that time. The story of that trip has been examined by many writers and has been the subject of numerous television and radio shows.

In 1944 Sergeant Larsen received orders to return from Halifax, on the east coast of Nova Scotia to Vancouver on the west coast of British Columbia, again via the Northwest Passage. The *St Roch* was to resupply RCMP posts on the way through the Passage.

The vessel left Halifax July 22, 1944, but had to put in at Sydney, Nova Scotia for mechanical repairs. She headed north out of Sydney July 26. On September 4, 1944 the *St Roch* anchored at Holman Island.

Fort Ross *finally home*.

We now take up the story in the Commander's own words from page 37 of his booklet:

"Shortly after noon, September 4th we anchored at Holman Island. I thought it strange that no one came to meet us, as there is a R.C. Mission, a Hudson's Bay Post and several natives there. A blast from our whistle brought no life whatever.

"When we went ashore we learned that the people had been up all night unloading supplies from the H.B.C vessel *Fort Ross*, which had left only a few hours before our arrival, and, tired out, they had been in bed. When awakened by our whistle they thought the *Fort Ross* had returned for some reason.:

"There more history was made, there two Canadian vessels had completely circumnavigated the North American Continent, the "*Fort Ross*" had left Halifax three months before us and had sailed through the Panama Canal, up the west coast to Vancouver, where she had been loaded for the western Arctic."

It is clear that the *Fort Ross*, heading east through the Passage, met the *St. Roch* heading west. It is also clear that Sergeant Larsen credits the *Fort Ross* with the circumnavigation in 1944. His reference to "two vessels" is a bit confusing and unclear since it is now accepted by many, that the *St. Roch* did not complete the circumnavigation from Vancouver, through the Panama Canal to Halifax, until 1950.

Fort Ross
Comes out of the Shadow

Addendum

History Updated

by Roger McAfee

Research into the *Fort Ross* for this update led me to the conclusion there is an arguable case to be made that *Fort Ross* was the first Canadian vessel to transit the Northwest Passage from west to east, thus also making it the first vessel in the world to circumnavigate North America.

The same research suggests Canada may soon be drawn into an international battle over Northwest Passage sovereignty and, hopefully, this Addendum will foster a useful discussion on that topic. That discussion inevitably involves two historic vessels. One is incredibly well known, and her day to day work in the Arctic has properly earned her the vast amount of fame and respect she has garnered. That vessel is the *St. Roch* and she is rightfully a Canadian National Historic site that lives on at Vancouver's Maritime Museum.

If Canada is successful in beating back claims that would impinge on the sovereignty Canadians have traditionally exercised over the Canadian Artic and particularly the Northwest Passage, it will be in large part, due to the heavy lifting that *St. Roch* and her RCMP crew did during their Arctic service.

However another vessel contributed greatly to that sovereignty and, until the writing of this Addendum, has been very much in the shadow of the *St. Roch*. That ship was a Hudson's Bay vessel *Fort Ross* and it's time for her to come out of that shadow.

When undertaking more research into the history of the *Fort Ross* I chose to, as much as possible, try to find evidence based on copies of original documentation. The Hudson's Bay Archives are in Winnipeg, as part of the Manitoba Provincial Archives, and is the best, but not the only, source for HBC history. Not wanting to spend time in Winnipeg's winter, I arranged for an independent researcher to search the archives and send me material related to *Fort Ross*.

It turned out that Library and Archives Canada also had material related to the *Fort Ross* and I obtained copies of what is there. I reviewed all the material I received and came to my own conclusions based on what I received. Some of the documents needed to be "interpreted" and those interpretations are mine and mine alone. Any errors are also mine and mine alone and are honest mistakes.

Since questions of Arctic sovereignty, particularly in the area of the Northwest Passage, are now often front and centre in the popular press, readers might like to have more information about the Arctic and the various attempts to find, and conquer, the Passage. For those so inclined I suggest a book – **Across The Top Of The World** – by Dr. James Delgado. He is a former Executive Director of the Vancouver Maritime Museum, and is well known, around the world, as an underwater archeologist.

While in this Addendum there is a discussion about only two vessels – *Fort Ross* and *St. Roch* – there were many other HBC vessels and trading posts as well as other police boats and land based police detachments that contributed substantially to Canada's claim for Arctic sovereignty.

Why the concern about Sovereignty?

Canada should be very concerned about sovereignty issues in the far north because both the British and American governments have adopted the position that if the Northwest Passage becomes regularly navigable it should be considered International waters. If that happens Canada will have no control over the types of vessels running through Canadian waters, and no control over the quality of the vessels, the cargos or the crews on board. Yet it's Canadian land and property that will be impacted and Canadians that will have to clean up any mess that might occur! If the Northwest Passage becomes international waters Canada will have absolutely no authority of any kind over the area. How long do you think it would take before Russia, or one of the other countries started "building" an island or some other permanent structure in the Passage?

China, as many who follow these things know, has already built, on Fiery Cross Reef, which has been described as "...a couple of rocks jutting out of the ocean at high tide..." in the

Fort Ross *servicing locals on one of her stops.*

South China Sea, about 3,200 acres of useable land. All other countries who are also claiming ownership in the Spratly Archipelago have added 50 acres in the same time frame. China is using the increased land base to advance its sovereignty claim and therefore take control over large areas of the South China Sea,

There is also the growing concern over countries like Russia, Denmark, Norway and the US. all claiming an interest in areas in the vicinity of the Geographical North Pole. In 2007 a Russian submarine planted a Russian flag on the ocean bottom at the Geographical North Pole. The ocean depth at that location is 4,000 meters or just more than13,100 feet. That location is in international waters and is about 500 miles toward Russia from the magnetic north pole. Various countries are anxious to stake a claim in Arctic waters because of the possibility of large gas, oil, and mineral deposits to say nothing of a potentially lucrative fishery.

Russia has gone to the UN claiming that, under UN Law of the Sea, its Arctic boundaries extend 350 miles out from the shore, adding about 450,000square miles to its territory.

Russian icebreakers and other Russian "research vessels" have been taking paying passengers into the Northwest Passage ice for a number of years. Vessels from all the countries that have easy access to waters above the Arctic Circle, are running Arctic cruises. These countries include Scotland, Iceland, Greenland, Norway and Sweden. Most of the ships used are, in various ways, ice hardened and carry about 250 passengers.

In the summer of 2016 a more "regular" cruise ship, after three years of planning, took on the Arctic and the Northwest Passage by successfully cruising from Anchorage, Alaska to New York. *Crystal Serenity* an 820 foot 68,870 ton luxury liner left Anchorage August 16 and arrived in New York 32 days later. It carried almost 1700 passengers and crew. It was accompanied by RRS *Ernest Shackelton* a class 5, double hull icebreaker. The cruise line has announced plans for a similar trip in 2017.

It is interesting to note that nowhere in the material related to that cruise is there any acknowledgement that the Northwest Passage is in Canadian waters. In promotional material the Northwest Passage is referred to as "…a mystical Pacific-Atlantic sea route far beyond the Arctic Circle that for centuries captured the imagination of kings, explorers and adventurers." It is interesting to note the Passage is referred to as the "sea route" between the Pacific and Atlantic, both international waterways.

At one point the material notes only that the ship will be passing "…through the Canadian Arctic Archipelago and on to Greenland."

If ships of this size, carrying 1,700 crew and passengers, start regularly using Arctic waterways, local services and infrastructure – safety, law enforcement, medical - would be overwhelmed if anything were to go wrong. For instance Nome, one of the larger communities along the route, has a population of just less than 3,600 inhabitants and has a total of only 18 hospital beds!

Traffic in the Arctic is increasing. Nome saw 35 dockings yearly throughout the 1990s and had just more than 730 last year (2015).

It has been suggested that ships be charged a fee to use the Passage, much like a Canal fee, and the funds raised be spent on infrastructure. However if the Passage becomes International waters, no country would have the jurisdiction to collect the fees and distribute the revenue.

What is Sovereignty?

Sovereignty is the ability of a State to absolutely control happenings within its borders without interference from another State.

We will try to keep this discussion as "non-legal" as possible, but some legal terms may sneak in. Sorry about that! We're going to talk about territorial sovereignty and the things that must be done for a country to successfully claim, or hold, this type of sovereignty right. The public is used to, and generally accepting of, the notion that a State occupies a particular piece of territory on the surface of the earth. While there are often border disputes between adjacent states, all countries can generally exercise their policies within their borders without interference from other States.

In order to establish one of the twin pillars of sovereignty a State must make use of the territory. "Making use of the territory" takes more than merely passing over it, or sailing through it or going under it if in a submarine. It takes exploitation of a resource and in the case of the Arctic, the Hudson's Bay Company started exploiting Arctic resources even prior to its incorporation in 1670.

That company engaged in a very lucrative fur trade from its outset and when it sold all eight million square kilometers of its land to Canada, for $1.5 million, in 1869, all of the value of the work, and benefits derived from the two centuries of HBC use of the land, remained attached to the land and came to the Canadian Federal Government.

As an aside, it is not widely known that the Americans, feeling pretty good after their successful acquisition of Alaska from the Russians for $7.2 million in 1867, the year of Canadian Confederation, were looking to expand and eyeing the HBC territory. One also has to remember that the U.S. had, in 1803, purchased 827,000 square miles of territory west of the Mississippi River from France for $15 million. Expansion of U.S. territory, by purchase, was a well developed American strategy at the time.

Clearly the *Fort Ross* was heavily and continuously, during her time as an HBC vessel, involved in making use of the resources of the territory. She brought HBC trading posts the supplies and trading goods needed to carry on business and took the furs to major population centers. She was therefore one of the two pillars required to establish territorial sovereignty. *Fort Ross* also performed another function in helping to establish northern sovereignty. She served as a mobile air service base for many of the aircraft that regularly made use of the Arctic air space. See the photo on page 15.

Aircraft sought out, and landed near the vessel, because she could provide warmth, a good bed, food and a meeting place for the pilots, crew and HBC or government officials. She could also provide fuel for the planes themselves. The regular use of Arctic air space strengthens Canada's sovereignty argument.

The second pillar of territorial sovereignty is the bringing of law and order and government services to the land over which sovereignty

	RECORD OF VESSELS AND BARGES					
	DETAILS OF OPERATION					
NAME OF VESSEL "Fort Ross"				DISTRICT	We	
			Hours Run	Fuel		
Year	Details of Operation			Diesel and Gas		
				Gals. Fuel	Gals. Lub.	Wo Co
1938	Lunenberg, Panama, Vancouver Unalaska, Coppermine, Bernard H.		1356	14,670	436	
1939	Bernard Tuktuk Herschel Tuk Perry Tuktuk Coppermine Tuktuk		516	5,080	152	

is sought. The heavy lifting of this pillar was done by the *St. Roch*. The work performed by the *St. Roch* and her RCMP crew can best be summed up in the words of the ship's commander, Sergeant (as he was then) Henry Larsen. He outlined, on page 3 of his booklet **"THE NORTH-WEST PASSAGE 1940-1942 AND 1944,"** their duties while in the Arctic: "… to act as administrators for the North-West Territories Council; maintaining game laws; making general check ups of Eskimos' living conditions; compiling Vital Statistics; authorizing the issue of rations for destitute age and infirm Eskimos; taking of census; settling of any disputes which might arise; conveying children to and from the residential schools at Aklavik; and transferring sick Eskimos for treatment and hospitalization at Aklavik."

Then of course there was the normal police work required of a regular RCMP detachment. There was also the constant work required to keep the floating detachment ship shape.

Clearly, at least as far as Canadians are concerned, the two vessels, between them firmly established Canadian sovereignty over the Arctic and particularly the territory containing the Northwest Passage. We would argue that under International Law Canada has established Sovereignty over the territory in question. We would also point out that until very recently nobody seriously challenged that status. If Canada is able to beat back the recent detractors, it will be because of the grinding, day to day, work of vessels like *Fort Ross* and *St. Roch*, and their crews.

How To Determine A Ship's Position.

In this day and age, it's relatively easy to pinpoint a ship's position. We can look at radar tracks or at GPS trackers and see, almost to within 100 feet, where a vessel has been and when, almost to the second, it is was at that location. Such was not the case in the 1930s and 1940s and while radar was being developed it was still in experimental labs.

In the time frame we are talking about in this book there was really only one way to determine where a vessel had been at any given time – and that was to examine the ship's papers, including log books, But even that process comes with a couple of caveats. The first is whether or not the keeping of a log book was a mandatory required duty of those running the ship. Military ships were almost certainly required to keep log books. Quasi-military ships – those used by law enforcement, coastguard, marine rescue, were likely to be required to use log books. General trading vessels may or may not be required to use log books.

The second caveat is whether or not entries in the log were made contemporaneously with the events as they happened. In others words if a log book entry show the vessel "…off White Point at 5:45 pm…" was that entry made at 5:45 pm as the vessel was, in fact, off White Point? Or was the logbook entry made sometime later and based on memory as to the time the vessel was off White Point? An examination of other entries in the log books will be

---

Y

THE BRITISH CORPORATION REGISTER OF
SHIPPING AND AIRCRAFT

ANNUAL SURVEY

Motor Vessel "FORT ROSS" of Winnipeg, 272 Tons gross Register

THIS IS TO CERTIFY that J. Forbes ---------------------
the undersigned surveyor to this Society, did at the request of the Owners,
Messrs. Hudson's Bay Co., attend the wood motor vessel "FORT ROSS" of
Winnipeg, 272 Tons Gross Register, as she lay afloat and on Dry Dock at *at Tuktuk?*
St. John's Newfoundland, on the 4th day of April 1942, and subsequent
dates, in order to survey the vessel in accordance with the Rules of the
Society for annual survey.

The vessel was placed on the Dry Dock at St. John's,
Newfoundland.

Examined Keel, stem and stern posts, sheathing, bow protection plates
and hull planking, *as far as seen afloat.*
Examined rudder and fittings, decks, bulwarks, hatches and hatch coamings,
covers and tarpaulins and wedges and battens fore and afters, beams, knees,
ceiling, timbers and bulkheads.
Examined Masts and rigging.
Examined ventilators, freeing ports, doors, coamings and all openings
to Crew's quarters, engine room, saloon and galley.
Examined and tested Steering gear.
Examined windlass, hawse pipes and anchors.
Chain cables ranged and examined.
Examined Pumps and piping.
Verified load line marks. *(as shown on loadline certificate)*

MACHINERY

Main engine cylinders opened and examined.
Pistons, crosshead, pins and bearings, crank and main bearings examined.
Air Tanks examined externally and working pressure pumped up and safety
valves examined.
Sea connections opened and examined and closed in order.
Main Engines closed and tried out under working conditions.
Auxiliary machinery opened, examined, closed and tried out under working
conditions.
Propeller and outer and inner ends of stern tube examined.
Examined Fuel Tanks externally.
Examined all valves, pipes and connections.
Examined electric installations.

Repairs effected

Several bow protection plates refastened.
20 feet of false keel renewed.
Propeller nut removed and new nut fitted in place complete with keeper.
Hull painted.

In view of this annual condition survey, I am of the opinion that
this vessel isin a good condition and eleigible to remain as now classed
in the Register with fresh record of survey.

A S 5 42 St. John's, Newfoundland.

St. John's, Newfoundland, May 12th, 1942.

SGD. J Forbes
SURVEYOR

- 2 -

5. POSITION OF M.V. "FORT ROSS" AT MAY, 1944

  (a) British Corporation's letter of 18th May, 1944, gives the position as follows:

    (i) Special Survey No. 1 recorded as being completed in drydock at St. John's, Nfld., in April, 1942, with remaining requirements being carried out afloat at Montreal in May, 1942.

    (ii) In April, 1944, their Mr. Forbes carried out a practically complete Special Survey which he described as Special Periodical Survey No. 1, being presumably unaware that this survey had been recorded as already completed.

    (iii) In view of (ii), British Corporation are recommending to their Head Office that a new load line certificate be issued dating from April, 1944, to supercede the existing one which expires in May, 1946, and to remain in effect during the period of service in the Arctic.

  (b) The Fort Ross will, therefore, not have to come out to get a new load line certificate by May, 1946.

  (c) Fort Ross' next special survey, i.e. Special Periodical Survey No. 2, apparently still falls due in May, 1946. In view, however, of the April, 1944, survey being a practically complete Special Survey, and in view of the fact that the British Corporation are going to give her a new load line certificate to remain in effect during the period of service in the Arctic, it appears that the April, 1944, survey will be regarded as a satisfactory substitute for the Special Periodical Survey No. 2, due in May, 1946.

  (d) British Corporation would like us to arrange for the Fort Ross' officers to carry out, during lay up, all surveys with the exception of those necessitating drydocking.

    They would also like us to arrange that reports covering all such inspections, winter overhauls and repairs are prepared, signed by our responsible representatives and forwarded to their Montreal office for transmission to Great Britain.

    They remind us that in order to maintain the freeboard assigned to the ship, no reduction should be made in any of the conditions of assignment listed in the Annual Survey section of the pages from the "Ship and Machinery Rules" which they sent us.

    They also strongly recommend that sufficient spares be provided to keep all of these items up to the required standards throughout the period of service in the Arctic.

WINNIPEG, 19th May, 1944.
DR/SSG

The HBC archives material in Winnipeg, placed the vessel in the western arctic in 1940 and then on the east coast in 1941 but material did not show anything other than the year. It did not show when, or from where, the vessel left for the east coast, nor did it show which east coast port it was heading for, and when it arrived at that port.

However the material from the Library and Archives of Canada gave more detail and provided other ship's papers that were useful in pinpointing a vessel's location at a point in time. Two of the most useful in dealing with *Fort Ross* records are entitled **Agreement And Account Of Crew** and **Agreement And List Of The Crew**. These are pre-printed form documents, which seem to be used interchangeably. The words "… And Account Of Crew" used in the title of the document does not mean the crew gives their version of happenings. It means how much they were to be paid.

helpful in determining how log book entries were made.

If a log book was properly kept and it gave a vessel's location at a given date and time, one could reasonably rely on the log book entry as fact.

When looking into this matter it became apparent there was a very short period of time that needed to be accounted for – the year 1941.

An Agreement And List Of The Crew places the *Fort Ross* at Vancouver, B.C. on April 2, 1941. The Agreement provided that the crew was signing on for a voyage from "Vancouver, British Columbia, thence to any Port or Ports on the Atlantic seaboard of the Dominion of Canada, for a period not exceeding twelve (12) months. Final port of Discharge, St Johns Newfoundland." The Agreement also notes that "Port at which Voyage Commenced

Fort Ross off Cape Chidley with Captain Dawe on the bridge wing.

Vancouver B.C." The Agreement was witnessed by Ralph Summers, Master of the vessel.

Ship's papers place the *Fort Ross* at St Johns, Newfoundland June 16, 1941, 75 days after leaving Vancouver. It should be noted that the Vancouver crew signed on for 12 months. It should also be noted that when *Fort Ross* came from the east coast to Vancouver through Panama in 1938 the trip took 32 days.

There are no *Fort Ross* official log books currently available in the Winnipeg Archives prior to 1947. There are log books for the years 1939, 1940 and 1944 in Library and Archives Canada. There is, at the present time, no log books for 1941, 1942, 1943, 1945 and 1946 and there is no way to know whether that was because the vessel did not keep an official log for those years or whether the log books have simply been lost over time. It's likely they have been lost or misplaced and may show up as more research is done. If the log books were available it would be easier, subject to the caveats noted above, to establish with some level of certainty where the *Fort Ross* was at any given time. It is also possible the logs for those years – WW II years – were destroyed by military order.

When attending law school at the University of B.C. almost half a century ago, one of the best law professors there taught evidence. He used to remind us that: "He who needs a fact must prove it."

I've decided, as we go forward in the discussion about the *Fort Ross*, the Northwest Passage and the circumnavigation of North America to use the same approach. It should be noted that the numbers and letters appearing in brackets in the "evidence" portion of what follows is the Hudson's Bay Archives identifiers.

Facts needed:
Fort Ross sails from east coast through Panama, to west coast and the Arctic;

Evidence:
Fort Ross launching photos Daysprings Nova Scotia and report in **The Beaver** September 1938, page 59. Photos of that launching also appear in this book.

Fort Ross travels from Nova Scotia, through Panama to Vancouver and then on to the Arctic to Unalaska, Coppermine and Bernard Harbour. A document from the HBC archives entitled **Record Of Vessels And Barges Details Of Operations**, a document kept in the ordinary course of HBC business, shows that in 1938 the *Fort Ross* went to the Western Arctic via "… Lunenberg, Panama, Vancouver, Unalaska Coppermine, Bernard H…" The document shows us the vessel required 1,356 engine hours to do the trip. It also shows the vessel burned 14,670 gallons of fuel and used 436 gallons of lube oil. (RG3/51/18).

The September 1938 #2 of **The Beaver** (the HBC employee magazine) reported as follows:

"Our new *Fort Ross* sailed in ballast from Lunenberg, N.S. on June 18 and arrived at Balboa, in the Canal Zone, on June 30, covering a distance of 2,450 miles at an average speed of 8.6 knots. The master of the ship reported that the vessel proved satisfactory under all conditions. After clearing the Panama Canal, the ship sailed for San Pedro, covering the 2,939 miles at an average speed of 9.2 knots, docking at San Pedro on July 14. Fine weather was encountered on this stage of the voyage.

The *Fort Ross* then proceeded, on July 14 on the last leg of her journey from San Pedro to Vancouver, a distance of 1,170 miles. The average speed for here was only 6.9 knots, heavy headwinds greatly diminishing the speed. The journey from Lunenberg via the Panama Canal to Vancouver was successfully accomplished in thirty two days, well ahead of schedule. The total of 6,600 miles was made with an average speed of 8.5 knots."

More evidence of this same passage is found in a 2014 article by George Dudley about a vessel, the *Audry B*, a former Arctic supply ship that carried freight for the HBC before turning to more profitable rum running and liquor smuggling into the United States.

The author says "*Fort Ross* was constructed in Nova Scotia and arrived in the Western Arctic in the late summer of 1938 via the Panama Canal and the west coast. It carried a full load of supplies from Vancouver".

Facts Needed:
Fort Ross operates as an Arctic supply ship:

Evidence:
Operating results in the Western Arctic 1938/39 7,411.84 (RG7/8A/99). The document referred to above, **Record Of Vessels And Barges** shows that in 1939 *Fort Ross* shuttled back and forth among trading posts in Bernard Harbour, Tuktuk, Perry,Tuktuk,Coppermine and Tuktuk. The records show engine hours run were 516 and fuel burn as 5,080 gallons. The engine consumed 152 gallons of lube oil that season.

On September 14, 1940, an HBC employee, W Gibson wrote to R.H. Chesshire, HBCs Fur Trade department manager noting...

"The delivery of the Annual Supplies from Tuktuk was carried out expeditiously by the *Fort Ross* on what constituted a record run." The letter goes on to say "...naturally I would like to visit Tuktuk during the early summer and accompany the *Fort Ross* eastwards." (RG7/1/1885)

Given that Gibson's letter was written in September of 1940 he was clearly talking about wanting to accompany "...*Fort Ross* eastwards" in the summer of 1941.

Facts needed:

Fort Ross arrives on the east coast in 1941 thus, assuming it arrived there via the Northwest Passage (an arguable point), completing the world's first circumnavigation of North America and becoming the first Canadian vessel in history to transit the Northwest Passage from west to east.

Evidence:

As noted above, on April 2, 1941 *Fort Ross* ship's paper establish the vessel was in Vancouver signing on a crew for a trip, "...not exceeding twelve (12) months." to St. Johns, Newfoundland.

As also noted above, 75 days later, June 16, 1941 *Fort Ross* was in St. Johns, Newfoundland, where she signed on a crew for a six month voyage "...St. Johns to and from ports and places in Newfoundland and ports and places in the Dominion of Canada..."

Further confirmation of the *Fort Ross* presence on the east coast is available by two HBC Archives photographs taken from the vessel

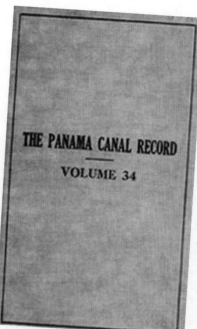

itself (Archive numbered 1987/363-F-55/50 and 1987/363-F-55/51) one off Cape Chidley, the northern most point of Labrador, and another off Table Hill, about 175 miles south. They appear at pages 115 and 118 of this book.

Some writers have assumed *Fort Ross* came to the east coast to "fill in" for the *Fort Garry* another HBC supply ship, and their assumption is understandable since many of the *Fort Garry* crew were on *Fort Ross* once she appeared on the east coast.

In fact there, so far, has been no evidence that the *Fort Ross* replaced the *Fort Garry* . In fact the U.S. War Department Quartermaster's Corps on March 18, 1943 was enquiring about the *Fort Ross* itinerary. In a letter dated July, 19, 1943, the Hudson's Bay Company sent a revised itinerary to the then Canadian Assistant Under Secretary of State, advising the original itinerary had to be changed since *Fort Ross* was assisting another HBC supply vessel, the *Nascopie*, because that vessel was experiencing serious boiler problems and had not been able to complete her most northerly calls the year before.

It is likely the real reason *Fort Ross* came to the east coast was to have a survey for classification purposes. It has to be remembered that the vessel was registered as a British vessel under **The British Corporation Register Of Shipping And Aircraft** and a British surveyor

Fort Ross off Cape Mugford, 175 miles south of Cape Chidley.

was required to do the survey. The only place in North America where a British surveyor could be found was in Newfoundland which, until 1949, was a British Crown Colony. The survey certificate, found at page 114 was signed by a "J Forbes" May 12, 1942. The same survey is referred to in a letter between two HBC departments June 19, 1944.

Unfortunately there is no official *Fort Ross* log book for 1941 so we don't know what route the vessel took from Vancouver to St. Johns. There are, however, only two possibilities – the Panama Canal or the Northwest Passage.

Through The Canal?

If the vessel went east through the canal, one would expect to find evidence of that transit in the **Panama Canal Record**, a publication that noted, by name and type of ship, the various vessels using the Canal. The last edition of that publication, Volume 34, appears to have recorded vessels going through between August 15, 1940 and April 30, 1941 and the *Fort Ross* does not show as having gone through the canal during that time frame.

One could argue the vessel went through the canal after April 30, 1941. The problem with that argument is we have the vessel leaving from Vancouver for the east coast April 2, 1941. It would have taken 20 days for it to reach the canal, based on the time it took for the vessel to go from east to west through the Canal to Vancouver in 1938. Remember the vessel encountered strong head winds heading north on that trip. Assuming the same speed going south *Fort Ross* would have arrived at the canal April 22, 1941 eight days before the end of the time covered by Vol 34 of the Record.

The Agreement And List Of The Crew document of April 2, 1941, referred to above, reveals the crew signed on for 12 months. If the vessel had intended to return to the east coast via Panama why would it have signed on a crew for a full year, when the 1938 trip through Panama to Vancouver was completed in only 32 days?

Through The Passage?

What facts are there that might support the argument *Fort Ross* went to the east coast in 1941 via the Northwest Passage? As noted above, the crew signed on for 12 months, a realistic time frame for a northern bash through the Passage.

Hudson's Bay Company ship captains were very familiar with the Arctic waters and they ran ships that serviced both the western Arctic and eastern Arctic. The western Arctic was serviced out of Vancouver and the eastern Arctic out of Halifax and St. Johns, Newfoundland. It would not be a stretch to assume captains servicing the eastern Arctic would meet with captains servicing the western Arctic.

In fact Anthony Dalton, one of the most knowl-

edgeable marine writers when it comes to HBC ships, and a regular seminar presenter at the Vancouver International Boat Show, writes about such a meeting. He recounts in his book **The Fur-Trade Fleet: Shipwrecks of the Hudson's Bay Company** a 1937 meeting at the HBC trading post at *Fort Ross*, on the east shores of the Boothia Peninsula of two HBC vessels. *Aklavik* came from the west and *Nascopie* came from the east.

He goes on to say, at page 125, "With that historic meeting two HBC ships had bridged the Northwest Passage." It has to be remembered that HBC crews did not see themselves as doing anything extraordinary as they went about their day to day work. They did not see themselves in the historical context we now do. They were probably more concerned about how good the food was and when could they get home to their families – the same things those working away from home think about today!

One cannot talk about the Northwest Passage, or anywhere in the Arctic, without consideration of ice conditions. It appears that some

Fort Ross in 2011.
Photo by Ann McAfee.

years were "good ice years" when shipping moved relatively unimpeded by ice. Other years can be "bad ice years" when iced blocks most of, if not all, navigable waters.

It should also be noted from the letter of September 14, 1940 referred to earlier must have been a "good ice year" since *Fort Ross* delivered the annual supplies "…on what constituted a record run."

Reliable research into Arctic ice conditions in the late 1930s and early 1940s is difficult because of the ongoing battle about climate change but both sides in that argument seem to agree that between 1938 and 1943 there was a substantial "melt" in the Arctic. In fact in the December 1938 edition of **The Beaver** we find the following "The season had been an open one on the coast and no difficulties were experienced with ice, which is a welcome contrast to previous years."

We also have some reliable information on ice conditions from Henry Larsen of *St. Roch*. Larsen left Vancouver June 23, 1940 and arrived in Halifax October 11, 1942, 28 months later. The return trip – Halifax to Vancouver - was done in 86 days – July 22, 1944 to October 16, 1944 - even though the vessel took a more northern route when steaming west. Larsen, at page 42 of his booklet, noted in discussing the 86 day east to west transit, "During that time we had only steamed 1031 hours and 34 minutes." That was 42.97 days. Let's round up to 43 days. Clearly some years in the early 1940s were "good" ice years.

There is another source of information related to Arctic ice conditions in the 1930s and 40s. The Arctic Circle, an informal group of influential Canadians involved in the Arctic, published a newsletter, **The Arctic Circular**, related to Arctic matters. Vol. II No.1 January 1, 1949 contains material that is helpful in discussing changing ice conditions in the Arctic.

It seems that ice from the Northeast Passage – a passage going east around Norway – became ice free in the early 1940s. The seas around Greenland, which had frequently been blocked with pack ice were almost ice free in 1931-33.

In the 10 years from 1907 to 1917 coal mines in Spitsbergen, northernmost Norway, were able to load coal onto ships for 92 days a year. By 1937, a mere 20 years later, they were able to load for 192 days a year. In 1878-80 the *Vega* was the first ship to navigate the Northeast Passage but it had to winter twice. In 1936 a flotilla of 14 Russian ships made the same transit in one season without ice problems. During World War II the Russians received millions of tons of war supplies required to fight the Germans by ship convoys through the Northeast Passage on what became known as the Murmansk Run. The route was ice free.

When Larsen completed his 1944 east to west accomplishment, he mused about the various earlier unsuccessful attempts by others to transit the Passage. On page 42 of his booklet we find: "It is true that many pioneers were defeated by the North; but I think it was because of the snow and cumbersome ships of those days, rather than the ice and inhospitableness of the land. Ships at that time were powered mostly by sails or inadequate steam engines and when winter held them in a frozen berth there was often a crew of over a hundred to be fed."

He then goes on, at page 43, to say: "I believe

that before long the Arctic will become better known. Large powerful steel icebreakers driven by diesel motors will ply its waters and during the summer will carry supplies to the northern inhabitants; while planes will maintain regular flights over this area, summer and winter."

Still on page 43 he goes on to say: "But one thing is certain: modern ships will have the advantage in power and strength, and if held up will merely have to wait until a little later in the season. To future Arctic vessels, the young ice that forms even in open calm waters and which stopped us many times will present no obstacle. They will plow right through it."

Larsen's suggestion of the qualities of a successful Northwest Passagemaker could certainly fit *Fort Ross*. It was bigger, in both length and beam than *St. Roch* and powered by a 240 HP diesel, compared to *St. Roch*'s 150 HP diesel main (when launched) and she was 10 years newer. While she was still built of wood, she had a 5/8" steel plate layover at both the bow and the stern. *Fort Ross* was faster than *St. Roch* whose top speed was 8 knots. Even after a new 300 HP engine was installed in a 1944 refit, top speed was still only 8 knots! Economical cruise was 6 knots. *Fort Ross*, on the other hand had a top speed of in excess of 9.5 knots. The difference in speed is not surprising when one remembers *Fort Ross* was designed by the designer of the speedy, and famous, Bluenose.

Argument:
It is submitted there is no real question about the *Fort Ross* leaving the east coast and arriving on the west coast, via the Panama Canal in 1938 thereby completing more than half of the circumnavigation of North America. The evidence is conclusive and independent. There is also no question about the *Fort Ross* operating in the Arctic in 1938 and 1940. Note the letter of September 14, 1940 referred to earlier in this Addendum.

The other item to be noted in that same letter is the comment that Gibson "…. would like to visit Tuktuk during the early summer and accompany the *Fort Ross* "eastwards." It seems clear from that statement there were plans for the *Fort Ross* to go "eastwards" from Tuktuk, in 1941. "Eastwards" from Tuktuk would mean the vessel would have to transit the Passage to get to the east coast.

It is also argued that the fact the vessel was on the east coast in 1941 through to 1944 has also been proven beyond a reasonable doubt.

Readers will certainly have by now noticed a weakness in my fact pattern - the lack of documentation tracking the *Fort Ross* from the Pacific to the Atlantic. Some may feel that there must be some record, somewhere, of the *Fort Ross* stopping for fuel, perhaps at one of the HBC trading posts, as she came through the Passage. So far no such record has ever been found.

However one has to remember the vessel fuel tanks, as built, had a capacity of 6,500 Imperial gallons, which, based on her known fuel burn, gave her a range of almost 6,000 nautical miles, more than enough to come through the 1,620 mile passage – the distance from the major HBC supply depot at Tuktoyaktuk, in the west, and Pangnirtang in the east. The vessel, being a small freighter, was also capable of carrying hundreds of extra drums of fuel. When we brought the boat back in 1969 we carried 250 drums of diesel as ballast in the hold and on deck , There was room for more. While the lack of a record of the *Fort Ross* stopping for fuel is easily explained, there is one thing that has caused me concern - there is no record of the vessel contacting anyone on its ship to shore radio. The reason for that does not come to light until we learn that in 1944 the HBC applied to the government for "…a relaxation normal WT (wireless transmission-ed) silence instructions…" for the *Fort Ross* when she was in Arctic waters. Permission was granted for the *Fort Ross* to use "… ship to shore transmissions when the ship is north of parallel 65…"

Radio silence was in force in 1941 because of WWII, and not relaxed until 1944 and then only when the vessel was north of the Arctic Circle. On her trip through the Northwest Passage she was not permitted to use her radio and so did not contact anyone as she proceeded east. *Fort Ross* was equipped with a two way radio since 1938. The December 1938 edition of the **Beaver** we find, at page 60 "Radio communication is now an established fact throughout the Arctic…" "From the schooner *Fort Ross* we were able to contact by Radio RMS Nascopie, *Fort Ross* Post, Fort Severn at Repulse Bay, King William Land, Perry River, Cambridge Bay, and Tuktuk, a radius of approximately 750 miles."

And some readers may well feel that lack of "tracking" is fatal to my argument. But other factors should be taken into account. The vessel could have proceeded to the Atlantic via Panama, but there's absolutely no evidence she did that. In fact an examination of The Panama Canal Record, volume 34 shows no evidence of the *Fort Ross* transiting the Canal between August 15, 1940 and April 30, 1941. There are no copies of The Panama Canal Record currently available later than Volume 34.

When examining the issue of vessel transiting the Canal during the War years it has to be remembered that records of that time are not as reliable as they might have otherwise been due to war time security issues. It is possible, but unlikely, that the *Fort Ross* transited the Canal and was simply not recorded as having done so. Since the vessel was not a military ship that is not likely, but it is possible.

So that brings us to the question: How did *Fort Ross* get from the Pacific to the Atlantic in 1941? She most probably powered through the Northwest Passage. I argue that's precisely what she did.

So, in summary, it is argued that, on the balance of probabilities, and based on the research currently available, the evidence establishes that the *Fort Ross* was the first Canadian vessel to transit the Northwest Passage from west to east and the first ship to circumnavigate North America. I would hope that those who disagree with my conclusion will dig further into the matter, present their own conclusions and add to the growing body of information on the Canadian Arctic.

According to notes in the Arctic Circular, Vol 2 No. 1 1949 p 10 the *Fort Ross* Arctic service ended when she was replaced by a new vessel, *Fort Hearne* August 9, 1949. She returned to Vancouver where she was sold in 1950.

That brings us to the question of how *Fort Ross* got from the Pacific to the Atlantic in 1941. My view is that, given the evidence we have to date, the vessel probably reached the east coast via the Northwest Passage. If that is the case, *Fort Ross* would have been the first Canadian vessel to transit the Passage and the first one to circumnavigate North America. That is not the conventional wisdom at this point in time so I encourage anyone who does not agree with my conclusion to dig deeper into the matter, present their own research and conclusions and thus add to the growing body of information on the Canadian Arctic.

Some Random Thoughts

While puttering along doing research on *Fort Ross* other bits of information crossed one of my desk tops and I just can't pass up an opportunity to comment on a few of them.

HBC

It is clear that the Hudson's Bay Company, as I noted earlier in this book, has not been given the recognition it deserves for the role played in Arctic exploration and its contribution to Canadian sovereignty. It is fashionable among many academics and others who consider themselves to be the "conscience" of society to attack corporations founded with profit in mind. While they are certainly entitled to their own opinions, they are definitely not entitled to their own facts.

The undisputed facts are that a territorial sovereignty claim of the type raised by Canada has to be founded on the use of the territory claimed. The Hudson's Bay Company made more use of the Arctic and its resources than any other organized entity. That fact does not change because the pursuit of profit was the company's motive.

Dr. John Rae

Dr. John Rae was a medical doctor born in Scotland's Orkney Islands who signed on as an HBC ship doctor in 1883. He served as a medical officer at Moose Factory where he grew to know and respect many of the Aboriginal patients and their culture. He became an excellent hunter and quickly adopted the Aboriginal methods of travel and clothing.

In 1846 he became the first European to successfully winter in the Arctic without any supplies other than the animals he shot and the fish he caught. During the next ten years Rae led four Arctic expeditions one of which discovered the missing link in the mapping of the Northwest Passage. He also discovered the fate of the Franklin Expedition that was lost in 1847. Because he knew many others were searching for Franklin in the wrong place, he returned to England to communicate his findings to Lady Franklin and the British public.

Because much of his information came from the local Aboriginals, whom the British (including Franklin himself) considered "savages" and untrustworthy, his information went unheeded. Indeed Lady Franklin and her powerful British aristocratic friend succeeded in denigrating Rae and the information he brought. As a result of which he has never been given the credit he deserves for his incredible accomplishments. It also has to be noted that during the time Rae was exploring the Arctic he was in the employ of the Hudson's Bay Company who paid his wages and covered his expedition expenses. While people in the UK are slowly starting to recognize Rae's achievements, it would seem appropriate that Canadians should, in some formal way, recognize Rae's impact on Canadian Arctic sovereignty.

Sir John Franklin

It is clear from the evidence that Franklin was a disaster as a skipper and as an expedition leader. Clearly he was not overly endowed with brains either. He set out from England in two state of the art ships. He lost them both. A good skipper protects the safety of his crew.

Under Franklin's watch all his men died. He saw how the local Aboriginal people were able to survive but considered them, as did most British aristocrats of the day, to be "savages" and their culture "beneath" him. He learned nothing from their example.

Despite all of the above it is reported the Canadian government is planning to name one of the new ocean research vessels, currently being built in North Vancouver, after this disaster. It would seem more appropriate to name the vessel after someone like the late Dr. G.L. Pickard, one of the early heads of UBC's Institute of Oceanography.

Vancouver as an Arctic Supply Centre

Most Vancouver residents, even those who spend a lot of time on the water, have no idea Vancouver was the service centre for the Western Arctic. With Arctic tourism about to explode it seems that Vancouver should start letting the world know that if anyone wants to learn about the Arctic he or she should come to Vancouver. Vancouver is currently the starting port for thousands of people wanting to cruise to Alaska every year. Clearly if one wants to go north, to either Alaska or the Arctic, Vancouver is the place to start. Vancouver was one of the last stops made by *Crystal Serenity* before she started her historical, record breaking trip through the Northwest Passage.

Vancouver also has one of the best locations to do historical Arctic research – the Vancouver Maritime Museum. That museum is home to the world renowned *St. Roch* whose Arctic exploits are legendary, but not well known to the non-marine focussed public.

European countries have spent millions refloating old ships so they could become museum centre pieces. Sweden hauled up the *Vasa*, that sank in 1628 after sailing just more than one kilometer from where she was launched! It is one of Sweden's most popular tourist attractions drawing about three quarters of a million tourists a year.

A Norwegian group has just spent six years, and an undisclosed amount of money, lifting the late Roald Amundsen's *Maud* from its watery grave at Cambridge Bay, Nunavut. The ship sank in 1930. The plan is to get the vessel back to Norway where it will serve as a centre piece in a Museum.

The Vancouver Maritime Museum already has its centre piece and, unlike *Vasa* and *Maud*, *St. Roch* got to the museum on her own bottom after a lifetime of hard work. I'm not sure if that's a comment on the vessels or the skill of *St. Roch's* RCMP crews over the years, or both! Vancouver's connection to the *St. Roch* is a natural one. She was built in 1928, at North Vancouver's Burrard Dry Dock.

Franklin's abandoned derelicts

It appears that both of Sir John Franklin's abandoned ships – *Erebus* and *Terror* – have been found by Canadian searchers in Canadian waters. That brings up the question of the ownership of these abandoned derelicts that have been underwater for almost 170 years.

The British will, of course claim they own the derelicts, and all their contents. British museums are filled with items acquired by Brits of the past, without regard to title. It should be noted that the Brits gave up the search for the two ships more than a century ago.

The sad part is many Canadian officials, including some at Parks Canada, seem to accept the fact the derelicts belong to England. When doing research for this book I contacted the archeology people at Parks Canada and was told since the vessels were originally war ships, and Canada had an agreement about visiting warships, they belonged to Britain. I pointed out they were not warships, but rather ships trying to find a quicker and cheaper way to the riches of the East. That made those ships all commercial vessels.

The discussion ended with Parks Canada telling me they had an opinion from Canada's Department of Justice that the "ships" belonged to Britain. In email correspondence with Parks Canada I asked if that was the same Department of Justice that advised the Canadian government it had an airtight case in the prosecution of Senator Mike Duffy on 31 criminal charges. Parks Canada said it was.

The judge who presided over the Duffy trial properly acquitted Duffy on all 31 charges and had many unkind words about the government's case. As a former Vancouver City Prosecutor and a lawyer who had many dealings with DOJ I was not at all surprised by the outcome of that trial. I suggested Parks Canada get a legal opinion from some competent lawyers before allowing any part of the Franklin derelicts or their content, to be removed from Canada.

What should happen to the content of the derelicts? They should be put on permanent display in the only major Canadian maritime museum in that focusses on the Arctic – the Vancouver Maritime Museum.

Acknowledgement

At the recent Vancouver International Boat Show I was chatting with Peter Vassilopolous, the dean of west coast Marine writers. I was bemoaning the fact that, as part of the process of updating this book I was going to have to learn to use a new (to me) graphic design program so I could graphically upgrade the book's interior. Peter immediately offered to help. "Send me the print files and I'll modify the layouts for you," he said.

Peter has been in the writing and publishing business for more than four decades and has almost 60,000 marine guide books in circulation. Not only does he write and publish his own books, he continues to be a regular free lance contributor to Pacific Yachting magazine.

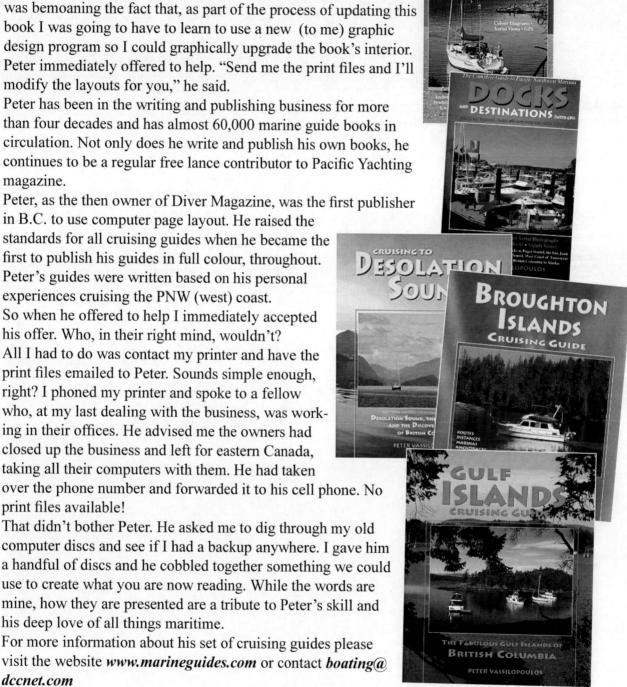

Peter, as the then owner of Diver Magazine, was the first publisher in B.C. to use computer page layout. He raised the standards for all cruising guides when he became the first to publish his guides in full colour, throughout. Peter's guides were written based on his personal experiences cruising the PNW (west) coast.

So when he offered to help I immediately accepted his offer. Who, in their right mind, wouldn't?

All I had to do was contact my printer and have the print files emailed to Peter. Sounds simple enough, right? I phoned my printer and spoke to a fellow who, at my last dealing with the business, was working in their offices. He advised me the owners had closed up the business and left for eastern Canada, taking all their computers with them. He had taken over the phone number and forwarded it to his cell phone. No print files available!

That didn't bother Peter. He asked me to dig through my old computer discs and see if I had a backup anywhere. I gave him a handful of discs and he cobbled together something we could use to create what you are now reading. While the words are mine, how they are presented are a tribute to Peter's skill and his deep love of all things maritime.

For more information about his set of cruising guides please visit the website ***www.marineguides.com*** or contact ***boating@ dccnet.com***